Retrospective Adventures
Forrest Reid: Author and Collector

WITHDRAWN

Retrospective Adventures

Forrest Reid: Author and Collector

edited by Paul Goldman and Brian Taylor

Scolar Press
in association with
Ashmolean Museum, Oxford

Published by
Scolar Press
Ashgate Publishing Limited
Gower House
Croft Road
Aldershot
Hampshire GU11 3HR
England

Ashgate Publishing Company
Old Post Road
Brookfield
Vermont 05036-9704
USA

in association with Ashmolean Museum, Oxford

British Library Cataloguing-in-Publication data
Retrospective Adventures
Forrest Reid: Author and Collector
1. Reid, Forrest, 1875 – 1947 2. Artists – Great
Britain – Biography 3 Authors, English – 20th
century – Biography
I. Goldman, Paul II. Taylor, Brian
700.9'2

Library of Congress Cataloging-in-Publication
data

Retrospective Adventures Forrest Reid: Author
and Collector edited by Paul Goldman / Brian
Taylor
ISBN 1-85928-463-9 (hb)
1. Reid, Forrest, 1875-1947 – Criticism and
interpretation. 2. Reid, Forrest, 1875-1947 –
Exhibitions. I. Goldman, Paul. II. Taylor, Brian.
PR6035.E43Z67 1998
823'.912--dc21   97-32019
                    CIP

Extracts from Theresa Whistler, *Imagination of the
Heart*, 1993, are reprinted by permission of Gerald
Duckworth & Co. Ltd.

Permission to quote from *The Collected Poems of
Walter de la Mare*, Faber and Faber, 1969, has been
granted by the literary trustees of Walter de la
Mare, and the Society of Authors as their
representative

Extracts from *Forrest Reid* by Russell Burlingham
and *Apostate* by Forrest Reid are reprinted by
permission of Faber and Faber

Hardback ISBN 1 85928 463 9 Scolar Press
Paperback ISBN 1 85444 008 X (Ashmolean
Museum)

Printed on acid-free paper

Typeset in Monotype Modern by Bryn Morgan
and printed in Great Britain
at the University Press, Cambridge

Contents

Foreword

In the *Annual Report of the Visitors of the Ashmolean* for 1946, K. T. Parker described the gift of the Forrest Reid collection in the following terms:

Presented by Mr Forrest Reid: A comprehensive collection, comprising many hundreds of items, of English wood-engraved book illustrations dating from about the 1860s, and including the work of some sixty artists, among whom are Rossetti, Millais, Whistler, Keene, Pinwell, &c. It is well known that in the early part of the second half of the nineteenth century English book-illustration passed through a period of extraordinary flower, during which much work of high quality and some of real genius and limpid beauty was produced. Mr Reid's collection, unique of its kind, is contained in a series of 33 solanders, each separate item being identified, dated, and mounted on card. It was used by him as the working material for his standard book *Illustrators of the Sixties*, published in 1928.
(pp.29–30)

Each of the thirty-three solanders contains some 150 illustrations, and the whole collection therefore numbers about seven hundred mounts. No correspondence survives to explain why Reid gave it to the Ashmolean, but the museum had had since the bequest of Mrs Thomas Combe in 1893 a notable collection of Pre-Raphaelite paintings and drawings, strengthened by gifts from the Burne-Jones family and Miss May Morris's bequest to the University of Oxford, in 1939, of William Morris's house, Kelmscott Manor, and the principal works of art it contained. Moreover, although Reid had no direct connection with Oxford, his friend and fellow Ulsterman, John Bryson, was a Fellow of Balliol and a discerning collector himself, and it was no doubt he who steered Reid's reference collection to the Ashmolean. The collection includes almost exclusively illustrations cut out of periodicals; Reid retained the illustrated books himself, and they passed to J. N. Hart, until they were sold by Sotheby's in 1965. The Ashmolean was bidding for several lots of prints in the same sale, and was unable to bid for the books, copies of most of which were already buried in the stacks of the Bodleian Library. No other British institution was interested, although several now regret the opportunity. The books were bought by Gordon Ray, and formed part of his bequest to the Pierpont Morgan Library in New York. Perhaps the two parts of Reid's collection might one day be temporarily reunited.

When I discovered that the small, grey solanders of Victorian wood-engravings had belonged to Forrest Reid (his name had long ago become detached from them), I asked Paul Goldman if he would be interested in preparing a small exhibition from the collection. He has done much more: with Brian Taylor, he has assembled a group of scholars to celebrate Reid's varied achievements, as a novelist, translator and literary critic as well as collector. The Ashmolean Museum is deeply grateful to them and to their fellow contributors, as we are to our friends at the Scolar Press, especially Pamela Edwardes and Sue Moore. Three charitable trusts have provided funds to assist with the publication: the Paul Mellon Centre for British Art, the British Academy, and the Esmé Mitchell Charitable Trust, Belfast. Without their help, there would have been no publication. The involvement of the last leads us to hope that the exhibition may be seen in Belfast, of which Reid was such a notable son.

Reid died in 1947, and both the exhibition and publication serve as a commemoration, albeit slightly belated, of the fiftieth anniversary of his death.

COLIN HARRISON
Oxford, 1997

Preface

The idea of holding an exhibition devoted to Reid's collection of magazine illustrations housed in the Ashmolean Museum was prompted by little more than the fact of the material having remained unknown and unexhibited for more than fifty years. Gradually, however, as a group of admirers of Reid gathered, the project turned into an attempt to review thoughtfully a writer, scholar and collector who has inexplicably and unjustifiably slipped from view. The result perhaps appears to encompass everything implied by the term 'inter-disciplinary' though indeed, in so many ways, this accurately describes Reid's numerous talents. As a novelist and an autobiographer he is almost without peer, in his innate grasp of the complex feelings and emotions engendered by male adolescence. In addition, as a literary stylist he continues to influence several of our finest contemporary writers. Hence the presence here of essays by John McGahern and Christopher Fitz-Simon. Other contributions, notably those by Robert Greacen and Anne Harvey, are more concerned with reminiscence and memory – activities which themselves play a significant part in Reid's own writing. Both offer a more personal perspective on Reid. Brian Taylor and Norman Vance reveal something of Reid's gifts as both creative artist and critic while Angela Thirlwell highlights the two very different volumes of autobiography. Reid's scholarship as an historian of nineteenth-century illustration is also acknowledged, while Robin de Beaumont examines the writer as a collector. The catalogue section can only hint at the richness contained in the collection in Oxford. Almost entirely removed from the magazines, it shows that Reid perceived correctly the central role played by the periodical press in providing vehicles for so many of the finest artists to display their talents.

Some years ago Lord David Cecil was asked which neglected writer deserved a reappraisal. His answer was Barbara Pym. As a result most of her books were re-published and she was fortunate to live to enjoy some of the recognition her talents so richly deserved. When Reid died in 1947 several of his books remained in print and his place in the world of letters seemed assured. Today, apart from a sporadic reissue, there is comparatively little of his work which is readily available to readers.

This book is now offered as a tribute to a writer who I believe warrants both revaluation and rediscovery. I am not alone in my opinion that both *Apostate* and *Uncle Stephen* could be termed, without hyperbole, 'modern classics', while not a few of Reid's other books could undoubtedly reward a contemporary readership. Perhaps if Reid is looked upon once more by both readers and publishers with something of the passion and the dedication of the contributors, then the present venture will have proved eminently worthwhile.

Paul Goldman
London 1997

A Chronology of Forrest Reid's Life

1875   Born 24 June at 20 Mount Charles in Belfast

1880   Family moves to 15 Mount Charles

1881   Father dies

1887   Attends Miss Hardy's Prep School, Cliftonpark

1888   Enters Royal Belfast Academical Institution ('Inst.')

1891   Leaves school, starts five-year apprenticeship at Musgrave's warehouse

1901   Mother dies

1904   *The Kingdom of Twilight*, London: T. Fisher Unwin

1905   Enters Cambridge University, October

   The Garden God: a tale of two boys, London: David Nutt

1907   Long vacation tour of Europe, visits Switzerland, Belgium, Paris and Bruges

1908   Leaves University, moves into 9 South Parade, Belfast, in November

1911   *The Bracknels: a family chronicle*, London: Edward Arnold

1912   Sends *The Bracknels* to E. M. Forster, meets Forster 13 February

   Following Darkness, London: Edward Arnold

1913   *The Gentle Lover: a comedy of middle age*, London: Edward Arnold

1914   Moves to 12 Fitzwilliam Avenue

1915   *W. B. Yeats: A critical study*, London: Martin Secker

   At the Door of the Gate, London: Edward Arnold

1916   *The Spring Song*, London: Edward Arnold

1917   Moves to 62 Dublin Road

1918   *A Garden by the Sea: Stories and sketches*, Dublin: The Talbot Press

1920   *Pirates of the Spring*, Dublin: The Talbot Press

   E. M. Forster's article on Reid, *Nation*, 10 April

1922   *Pender among the Residents*, London: Collins

1924   Moves to 13 Ormiston Crescent, July

1926   *Apostate*, London: Constable

1927   *Demophon: A traveller's tale*, London: Collins

1928   *Illustrators of the Sixties*, London: Faber & Gwyer; reprint (1975) New York: Dover Publications

1929   *Walter de la Mare: A critical study*, London: Faber & Faber

1931   Meets Stephen Gilbert

   Uncle Stephen, London: Faber & Faber

1934   *Brian Westby*, London: Faber & Faber

1936   *The Retreat; or, The Machinations of Henry*, London: Faber & Faber

1937   *Peter Waring*, London: Faber & Faber

1940   *Private Road*, London: Faber & Faber

1941   *Retrospective Adventures*, London: Faber & Faber

1942   *Notes and Impressions*, Newcastle, Co. Down: The Mourne Press

1943   *Poems from the Greek Anthology* (translated by Forrest Reid), London: Faber & Faber

1944   *Young Tom; or, Very Mixed Company*, London: Faber & Faber

1946   *The Milk of Paradise. Some thoughts on poetry*, London: Faber & Faber

1947   Dies at Warrenpoint, Co. Down, 4 January, buried at Dundonald Cemetery, Knock, Belfast, 6 January

   Denis Bracknel – A family Chronicle, London: Faber & Faber

1 Some Themes in the Novels of Forrest Reid

Brian Taylor

Forrest Reid wrote sixteen novels, two volumes of autobiography, two collections of short stories, critical studies of W. B. Yeats and Walter de la Mare, a definitive work on the book illustrators of the eighteen-sixties and numerous essays and book reviews.

The novels fall into two fairly distinct groups. The first includes the books written before the publication of his first volume of autobiography, *Apostate*, in 1926. These include his first published book *The Kingdom of Twilight* (1904), *The Garden God* (1905), *The Bracknels* (1911), *Following Darkness* (1912), *The Gentle Lover* (1913), *At the Door of the Gate* (1915), *The Spring Song* (1916), *Pirates of the Spring* (1919) and *Pender among the Residents* (1922). Of most of these, Reid himself had a low opinion, considering them 'false starts'. However, *Following Darkness* and *Pirates of the Spring* stand easily with his later and most accomplished writing. The second group of novels, in which Reid found his subject, the subject of youth and its adult recall, includes *Demophon* (1927), *Uncle Stephen* (1931), *Brian Westby* (1934), *The Retreat* (1936), *Peter Waring* (1937) – a reworking of *Following Darkness* (1912) – and *Young Tom* (1944).

Martin Linton, a writer in *Brian Westby*, is a thinly disguised portrait of Reid and Linton suggests to Brian Westby, who has been reading Linton's first novel, that 'it might be interesting to read the books in the order in which he wrote them . . . after a fashion, the books do fit together. I mean, he's got an ideal: and each of his books is an attempt to express it.'[1] Reid was always sure in his self-knowledge, in literary and other matters, but Linton's recommendation can only, sadly, be followed with difficulty by would-be readers of all of Reid's fiction. Of Reid's sixteen novels, and other books, a lifetime's work, only *Illustrators of the Sixties* and a handful of the novels are currently in print.

The notion that Reid used each of his novels to refine an informing ideal rather than expand his chosen subject is, however, a sound one. It is an exaggeration to claim, as some critics have done, that Reid could not create a believable character over the age of twelve, but there is a definite sense of a 'King Charles's head' in much of Reid's fiction – his adult characters are invariably less rounded than his juvenile ones. Graham Greene has noted that obsession lies at the heart of many modern writers, and a fruitful lead was provided by an anonymous *Times Literary Supplement* reviewer who suggested that 'E. M. Forster's heroes are the sort of men Forrest Reid's boys might have grown into, if Forrest Reid had allowed them to grow up'. Indeed, it was Forster, a friend of Reid's for many years, who, writing as early as 1920, went to the heart of the matter in words which hold their relevance today in his expectation that 'when his genius gains the recognition that has so strangely been withheld from it, he will be ranked with the artists who have preferred to see life steadily rather than to see it whole, and who have concentrated their regard upon a single point, a point which, when rightly focussed, may perhaps make all the surrounding landscape intelligible'.[2]

A common compliment paid to Forrest Reid during his lifetime was, as Russell Burlingham has noted, that he was the 'first Ulster novelist to achieve European status'. In a sense, the accolade is an unexpected one. The roads to literary fame are wide and are travelled by many, often more in hope than in the expectation of arrival. The road Reid travelled throughout a lifetime faithfully devoted to the cultivation and refinement of his art was always a private one, and it was the journey and not the arrival which mattered. Indeed, *Private Road* (1940) was the title Reid gave to his second volume of autobiography, and the name provides an apt title for an account of his literary career. To a biographer, Forrest Reid's life may seem something of a disappointment. He lived a simple, indeed a humdrum, sort of life. One of his commentators has noted that: 'Unlike so many writers who have turned their backs on the values of the contemporary world, living flamboyantly unconventional lives and enshrining in flamboyantly unconventional prose very ordinary notions, Forrest Reid spoke and wrote with grave simplicity about a system of values which, if adopted, would turn the world gently but firmly topsy-turvy.' How little interested Reid was in changing man's outward behaviour may be judged from his own quiet acceptance of provincial life, his disinclination to mingle in literary or political circles, his devotion to such unrevolutionary pastimes as bonfires, croquet, and jigsaw puzzles. As Reid himself observed, the external happenings of a man's life, when viewed in retrospect, are often few and sober enough. The adventure all along lies in their interpretation.

Reid was born the youngest of a family of six to Robert

Reid, a Belfast merchant, and to Frances Matilda Parr, a distant descendant of the last wife of Henry VIII. In the semi-rural Belfast of the 1880s, Reid's boyhood was by all accounts a happy one, though nowhere was Victorian morality more apparent than in the Presbyterian middle class into which he was born. Selected readings from improving literature on long dreary Sundays, a world of nurses and perambulators where children were constantly reminded that they should be seen and not heard – all of this should have produced a typical Victorian child. In Reid it brought on a strong reaction against religious orthodoxy and sent him on a life-long quest for a personal vision of paradise that, in all his subsequent writing, he strove to complete. Reid's external life and writing, then, were inextricably bound up with Belfast and with the surrounding countryside. The streets of Belfast, the shores of county Down, the brooding melancholy of the Mourne Mountains inspired and provided the setting for most of his novels, and the spirit of the river Lagan flows through them all. His landscapes are, for the most part, recognisably Ulster and his characters undeniably Northern Irish. The earliest novels – *Following Darkness* (1912), *At The Door of the Gate* (1915) and *The Spring Song* (1916) – clearly display a marked reliance upon local models for both their plots and their setting. With Reid's emergence into artistic maturity, however, his fiction turned into an amalgam of Ireland and Ancient Greece. It is, consequently, more difficult to place Reid's later novels, and particularly those comprising the self-acknowledged crown of his achievement, the Tom Barber trilogy, comprising *Uncle Stephen* (1931), *The Retreat* (1936) and *Young Tom* (1944). After *Apostate* (1926), Reid's prose is rooted in more fertile imaginative soil than that provided by the simple dependence on local colour.

And, as with *Apostate*, so with the novels. It is paradoxically true that Reid both excluded himself from the novels and included himself at a deeper level than that provided by mere plot or narrative. In this sense, *Apostate* may be regarded as a source for a life of a man whose impressions were recorded in the novels and not as itself a record of external events. For example, the character of Peter Waring, in Reid's novel of that name, is in no sense simply identifiable as Reid the author. Peter's interpretations of his experiences do bear, however, a marked similarity to Reid's own at the age of seventeen. Reid the artist, whose philosophy of art he called a 'crying for Elysium', utilised his novels to echo that idea rather than simply to repeat it. The difference between a repetition and an echo can also be seen to advantage in Reid's trilogy of novels dealing with the youthful character of Tom Barber. The first novel in that trilogy, *Uncle Stephen* (1931), concerns the adventures of the thirteen-year-old Tom. The subsequent two books – *The Retreat* (1936) and *Young Tom* (1944) – brought Tom's age to eleven and nine respectively. Reid, in fact, wrote the trilogy in reverse and his subject grew steadily younger as his creator grew older.

From the earliest novels, from Graham Iddesleigh's predilection in *The Garden God* to 'remember too much, remember in other words what never really was . . .', and the cautionary introductory note to *Peter Waring* that 'to return after an absence of nearly twenty years to a place beloved in childhood and boyhood is apt to prove a disillusioning experience', to the developed treatment of the theme of return in *Uncle Stephen*, the dominant note is one of going back, and essentially, of going home. *The Garden God* is a tale-within-a-tale, the mature Iddesleigh remembering 'what, alas! only might have been'; *Following Darkness* is constructed around Peter Waring's confusion as to precisely where 'going home' might lead him – to his unsympathetic father or to Mrs Carroll at Derryaghy House. Rex Pender's return to Ballycastle provides the spur to the events of *Pender among the Residents*; the whole of *Demophon* is concerned with Demophon's yearning for the companionship of his lost childhood friend translated into another journey home, and so on. Reid's notes for planned but unwritten stories also indicate this obsession. Sometimes these are short and enigmatic – 'story of a house haunted by the man himself. Lost river and contracting garden'. Sometimes they point, however briefly, to perennial concerns – 'story of a man revisiting a school, now abandoned, finds in a cupboard the skeleton of a boy who must have been there in his time . . . suddenly aware of the shade of one of the masters watching him – feels the only thing to be done is to bury the skeleton as quietly as possible'. And again, 'man comes after many years to old graveyard in Ballinderry – sees small boy and talks with him – come away together hand in hand – pass out through gate and the child gets farther and farther away. It is himself as he was – though only gradually he realises this'.

Closely allied to this theme of return is the theme of revision. The motive for going back, for going home, to the past or to childhood, in Reid's fiction is not the simple one of arrival at a yearned-for, less complicated, state of affairs. The whole purpose of return lies in the possibility of its revision. This is most obviously true of *Apostate*, less a reliable record of Reid's early years than a recreation of the necessary conditions for the man to which that child was father. Reid returned again and again to the years of his boyhood in his books – a goading recompense for personal loss. He returned to revise, to correct, to go over again the problems which he knew from his own boyhood, and to find somehow the answers which he never found there. Themes which recur repeatedly – themes of youth, of nature, of the supernatural – all had their origins in these early years but they only attained their power and importance in Reid's recollections of them. And what lay behind all of these themes was an overwhelming sense of the unlikelihood of attaining what one most desires, or, if it is fleetingly achieved, then the inevitability of its loss. Forster wrote once in a letter to Reid that 'your main activity is reconsideration – you are always turning over in your mind something that had happened long ago, and are hoping to find a more perfect expression of it than you have succeeded in finding'. Or, he might have added, than Reid ever did find.

All these themes are related in a developmental manner – they follow on, one from the other. The theme of return, of the obsession with boyhood as an icon of the fated impossibility of return, of revision, all are linked in Reid's own early experience. Revision was always present in Reid's manner of working, as well. Two of his novels, *Following Darkness* and *The Bracknels*, were wholly or partly revised, and Reid was contemplating a new version of *The Spring Song* during his last years. Always, and at all levels, there is this continuous emphasis on the need to get matters right. And in so doing, as Reid well knew, to find out what had gone wrong. The whole of *Apostate* is given over to this nagging question, this conviction that something at the beginning must have been different to account for the large divergences which Reid knew separated him from others as he grew up – or failed to. Reid's own diagnosis of what he called his 'mysterious case of arrested development' was, perhaps, not so very mysterious after all.

The theme of nature is allied to and runs through these concerns, particularly the love of animals. From those far-off days when he used to sally out for walks with Emma to feed the stone lions in University Square, from the days when the infant Forrest's affection was 'lavished on a stuffed black velvet elephant, who for years was my nightly bedfellow', the humanising impulse which prompted Reid's love of all forms of animal life remained with him. Like the Greeks whom he adored, he extended this feeling of community to the humblest creatures of the earth. Tom, in *Uncle Stephen*, hurrying along in the dusk on his first visit to Kilbarron, keeps his eyes on the ground lest he should inadvertently crush the snails in his path. The thought, and the touching idea behind it, are very typical of Reid. In the opening pages of Reid's typescript, the original draft has Tom fixing his attention 'on a creamy black-spotted butterfly which had entered the avenue'. In a later draft, the 'which' has been crossed out and replaced with 'who'. It is in *Young Tom* that Reid's approach to the animal kingdom is most clearly outlined. He even permits Tom's father to give it a name, the 'greater democracy'. Tom is unclear over this name, until Daddy explains that 'It means . . . a social community in which you and I and Tom, and squirrels and hedgehogs and dogs and mice, all have precisely equal rights to freedom and happiness – the communist ideal, in short; with this important difference, that it is to be extended to the non-human races . . . '[3]

Like most of Tom Barber's ideals, as with those of his creator, this one has a drawback; and Tom's plans for an aquarium have to be abandoned. Reid's treatment of animals is, in the truest sense, a humanist approach -

dogs, squirrels, cats, are never *de*humanised as in so much writing of this kind. The closeness to nature of Reid's fictional boy-heroes is evident in a common love of animals, not the sentimental exploitation of animals under the name of 'pets', but a recognition and acceptance of the animal's own life. When Demophon meets a centaur, he thinks at first that it is a ghost, but goes towards it. 'To tell the truth,' says Reid, 'if he had thought it to be a human ghost he would not have ventured near it – but the ghost of a beast could do no harm, since there is no such thing as an evil beast.' Unchanging affection, the absence of failure, the security of the past and regret at the onset of age and maturity; the connection is clear, and the coming together of all of these elements in the spirit of boyhood is consistent.

There is one other theme which remains to be considered. The sense of the supernatural runs through Reid's other preoccupations, but it is a special sense of otherness, peculiar almost to Reid alone. Compounded of the immanence of a world of underlying spiritual realities and its retrieval through the artistic manipulation of time and memory, Reid's version of the supernatural is at once strange and sincere. This supernatural quality, as he admitted himself, 'was inseparable from my conception of reality'. Not that this indicated an interest solely in ghosts or hauntings. What was meant was something altogether more spiritual. 'After all, a sense of the supernatural need not be accompanied by fear,' he once remarked. 'It may be aroused in broad sunlight – it may be no more than a suggestion of a deeper beauty, friendly and benevolent, existing behind the beauty of natural things. Such, at any rate, has been my own experience, and it was always a feeling unsought, a kind of expectancy, a state of mind far removed from dread.' This is the element which imbues his work with its spiritual quality, and this was the genre in which he shared mastery with Walter de la Mare. Sometimes, Reid permits this mastery to play nothing more than a decorative role in the novels. Into this category fall the activities of the magician Flamel in *The Gentle Lover*, and Rex's unconvincing ghostly memoir in *Pender among the Residents*. But more usually the supernatural theme is integral to the development of Reid's plots: Mr Bradley, the strange and mysterious organist in *The Spring Song*, the haunting of Denis in *The Bracknels*, and of course, the whole of *Uncle Stephen*, Reid's single most sustained achievement of this kind.

Perhaps Forrest Reid's most important book was one which, in the end, he never published. This was to be a novel called *The Green Avenue* and it was to deal with the theme of love in a more explicit way than he had ever attempted. The earliest mention of the book comes in letters which Reid wrote in 1928. It was to have been a school story; a boy is expelled because of his love for another. At home, an explorer or missionary friend of the boy's parents takes the matter lightly, but there is a deeper side to the affair. As the story progresses, it appears that what both parents and schoolmaster are really afraid of is not the suspected – and unproven – sexual contact but the growing realisation that the boy really is deeply in love with his friend. The title, as Stephen Gilbert has noted, was intended to indicate that while the avenue was green and attractive, the house, unseen from the gates, was a far less happy place. Stephen later asked Reid why he had not written the book and Reid told him that it was because he 'did not want to embarrass his friends'. Reid had written to the poet and writer Andre Raffalovich about this unwritten book. On 2 February 1928, Raffalovich had replied, 'I should not encourage you to give a year to *The Green Avenue* for fear of grieving all the many who love your former books.' And, he asked, 'Can't you use that strong impulse to write that book in giving a deeper bloom, more lustre, more of your core, to what you write? I think you should resist, but get something out of your resistance.' On the strength of the books which followed there seems little doubt that the advice was profitably taken. Forrest Reid's best work was always the result of this resistance. As in the avenue travelled by Tom Barber in *Uncle Stephen*, the gate had shut behind him:

Then he turned round and through the gate looked into the green avenue from which he had just emerged. Within there was something not so simple. While he lingered there deepened in him a strange impression that he was on the boundary-line between two worlds . . . Here he was free to choose, but if he took a step further all would be different. What he should enter seemed to him now a kind of dream-world, but once

inside, he knew it would become real . . . As he stood at the gate Tom at that moment wasn't very far from seeing an angel with a flaming sword guarding it. His body thrilled when the call of a bird rose through the silence. He took a little run forward, tugged at the bar, pushed: and the latch dropped back into place as the gate clanged behind him.[4]

The vision is near and always far away. As in the closing sentences of *Young Tom*, the vision is getting closer, the image becoming more and more real:

Next moment the darkness vanished, and he had a vision of a wide, curving beach of yellow sand, where children were playing in the sunlight at the edge of a timeless sea. They were building castles on the sand, and their happy voices reached him – gay, innocent, laughing. Vision or memory, the scene brought with it no feeling of strangeness, only the sense of returning to a lovely and familiar place, which would always be there, though at times it might be hidden from him . . . The dark blue water stretched out and out under a golden haze, till it met the softer, paler blue of the sky. That happy shore he knew – and it was drawing closer, it seemed very near, already less dream than reality. For he could feel the warm sun on his hands and face, and he had to step back quickly as a small wave curled over and broke, melting and hissing, in a thin line of foam at his feet . . . [5]

Notes

1. Forrest Reid, *Brian Westby*, London: Faber & Faber, 1934, p.25.
2. E. M. Forster, 'Forrest Reid', *Nation*, 19 April 1920. Reprinted in his *Abinger Harvest*, London: Edward Arnold, 1936, p.80.
3. Forrest Reid, *Young Tom*, London: Faber & Faber, 1944, p.121.
4. Forrest Reid, *Uncle Stephen*, London: Faber & Faber, 1931, p.111.
5. Forrest Reid, *Young Tom*, London: Faber & Faber, 1944, p.169.

2   Forrest Reid Remembered
Christopher Fitz-Simon

In the phrase of the chronically reminiscent, I cannot remember a time when I was unaware of the existence of Forrest Reid. Ours was not a 'literary' household when I was growing up in Ulster during the Second World War, but it was very much a 'reading' one. There was a weekly foray to the Carnegie Library; and the name of the celebrated Linenhall Library was constantly invoked by those intrepid enough to make the half-hour train journey to Belfast, the metropolis of our world. Forrest Reid's works stood in the bookcase between those of Thomas Mayne Reid – author of *Boy Hunters* and *Scalp Hunters*, and more than possibly a relation – and Erich Maria Remarque, whose *All Quiet On The Western Front* was much admired by my grandfather, an eminent surgeon of quizzical mien very much in the mould of Doctors Macrory and Birch. There were holidays at Newcastle, Co. Down; meetings and trysts of varying kinds took place in Belfast's Botanic Gardens; walks were taken along the Lagan tow-path to Shaw's Bridge, with or without a dog, depending upon the leader of the expedition; we were, whether we thought to identify the phenomenon or not, living in a kind of Reid theme park.

Indeed, Forrest Reid's name would be mentioned in tones of some reverence, as if he were a famous person known only to privileged older members of the family. I was not surprised, almost half a century later, when I learned that my kinsman, Stephen Gilbert, was his literary executor. Stephen Gilbert is also a distinguished novelist; his simple and poignant tale *Landslide*, set during a natural cataclysm in the west of Ireland, is one of those early-remembered books into which I still dip with frequency; it was, as I recall, the first 'adult' book I read to myself, when I must have been about ten. My initial conversations with Stephen Gilbert were occasioned by a commission from Radio Telefís Eireann to make Reid's *Bracknels* into a six-part serial. I had, by then, read all of Reid's prose fiction, and was concerned, in the irritating manner of those who make a practice of pillaging literature for quite unliterary reasons, with questions *à clef* regarding putative life-models for characters and locations. Stephen Gilbert answered with his customary courtesy; but ultimately the coarse considerations of actuality mean very little when one is dealing with imaginative writing: they merely serve as footnotes to one's own preconceptions.

'One of the three or four most distinguished living writers of English', the *Spectator* had declared in 1937. Comparisons were invited with E. M. Forster and, retrospectively, with Henry James. Yet to John McRae, who provided the introduction to the paperback edition of *Young Tom* half a century later, Reid was one of 'a number of writers whose reputations languish, awaiting critical rediscovery'. The ominous phrase 'undeservedly neglected' was one which I soon found to be applied by the compilers of literary guides, suggesting a coterie writer of irredeemably *passé* provenance; and during the course of my work it became clear that Forrest Reid's name meant nothing at all outside two small intersecting circles: academics specialising in the Georgian novel, and devotees of an idealised all-male world euphemistically described as 'Greek' yet unmistakably Victorian in general tendency. Two publishing events began the welcome process of Forrest Reid's reinstatement: the appearance of Brian Taylor's superb critical biography *The Green Avenue* in 1980, and the GMP reissues, edited by John McRae, later in the same decade.

In the Irish context, of course, it was perfectly natural that Reid's work should have become unfashionable, if it was ever quite fashionable. Irish novelists, dramatists and poets born between (say) 1850 and 1885 grew to be identified in one way or another with the Literary Revival, with – as in the case of Moore and Joyce, for example – associations of a more European drift. Reid had no part in any of this, either creatively or socially. Nor was he connected, either by temperament or tradition, with the members of the Irish 'big house' school of prose fiction, such as his contemporary Elizabeth Bowen. Even less was he connected with the post-Revival novelists like Frank O'Connor and Sean O'Faolain, who were coming to prominence by the time he had achieved critical acclaim. Furthermore, though he was acquainted with several of the Dublin writers, and though Dublin was only two hours away by train, the Irish capital was not the focus of his social life in the way that London would have been for a gregarious English writer living in Brighton or Cambridge.

Reid was far from gregarious. His few literary contacts were achieved more by correspondence than conversation, and with English rather than Irish authors. It is tempting, then, to place him as an 'English' novelist, for he certainly cannot be relegated to that deplorably damned category 'Anglo-Irish'. English in terms of sensibility, perhaps. Yet here again there is a difficulty, for certain elements – turns of phrase, the colloquial talk of country folk and city servants, and above all the luminous particularities of topography and landscape – are of Ulster. 'I don't mind seeing you in these parts before,' exclaims one of the rural characters in *Uncle Stephen*; 'You look well slept,' says another – phrases which could never be heard south of a line drawn from Carlingford Lough to Sligo Bay. In *Peter Waring* we are unmistakably in the foothills of the Mournes, not the Galtees or the Grampians or, for all Mrs Carroll's chintz covers and cushioned window-seats, the Cotswolds. An *Ulster* novelist, then? If so, he is unsurpassed; but it is an appellation which invites the ignominious taint of provinciality. Better leave it lamely at that, say that his work is *sui generis*, and agree gladly with Forster who said that all Forrest Reid's art was 'intensely personal, and stands apart from contemporary movements in literature'.

The critical deposit, from the publication of *The Kingdom of Twilight* in 1904 to that of *Denis Bracknel* (a revision of *The Bracknels*) in 1947, inclines heavily towards pre-eminence as an interpreter of childhood and adolescence: 'the sense of early wonder and adventurous boyhood . . .'; 'his illumination of boyhood, with all its sharpness and shyness, is as fragrant as a water-colour . . .' What has been lost on most of those commentators who can see little further than Reid's remarkable decipherment of *jeunesse perdue*, is his discreetly satiric delineation of the bourgeois society into which most of his young heroes have been born, and from which they are at pains to escape. The dreary philistinism of these suburban or provincial families is very keenly observed, particularly through the precociously perceptive eyes of Denis Bracknel, Peter Waring and Tom Barber, and, in a more detached way, by the older Hubert Rusk, whose view is tempered by the wry – albeit concerned – amusement of the outsider.

Detailed realism, supported by a subtly muted irony, combine to present an ethos of mild mockery which is somewhat at variance with the sombre introspection that pervades almost all of Reid's novel-writing, especially when these components are juxtaposed in one book. There is an imbalance of tone in *The Bracknels* and *Uncle Stephen*, as if the author had not been quite sure which line to take. By no means does it destroy the total effect, but it leads to questions of consistency. The scene where Amy Bracknel interrupts the tutorial between Hubert Rusk and her little brother Denis is one of hilariously subdued embarrassment, masterfully sensed and sustained; but it and others sit rather awkwardly beside the lengthy and beautifully composed passages of Denis's dark imaginings. In *Uncle Stephen* this dichotomy is more controlled, however. The dreadful high-tea which follows the funeral of Tom's father, when family resentments almost upset the gentility and forced solemnity of the occasion, is a superbly restrained comic set-piece which may be confidently compared to the famous Christmas dinner in *A Portrait of the Artist as a Young Man*; but a stylistic unease remains *vis-à-vis* certain lyrical passages when Tom enters his neo-classic dream-world. The latter are, of course, believable, in the context of the heightened perceptions of adolescence; and by this time in his career – technically as well as figuratively speaking – Reid was experienced enough to provide less jarring changes of gear.

If one were to persist in selecting and praising the realistic element in Forrest Reid's work, it would be to the unacceptable extent of overlooking his supreme achievement, which is the mapping of the lost demesnes of childhood. Yet there is no harm in indicating that other localities exist. At the same time, it is perhaps worth arguing that *Brian Westby*, an almost totally realistic novel – and clearly a very carefully structured one – is less 'interesting' than, say, *Uncle Stephen*, principally because of its capable consistency of style and outlook.

There are times when an almost sublime fusion of mode and material takes place, when the writer is in perfect control of his gift and its formulation. One example is enough, and is to be found in scenes in *Uncle Stephen* where Tom Barber, fresh from well-to-do and well-tutored suburbia, meets the rustic ne'er-do-well youth, Jim Deverell – first on a lonely road by a river, later in the density of the Kilbarron Manor woods, and finally in the cabin where Jim dwells with his mother, and from which he has to flee from the law with the help of money donated by young Tom. The edginess of what hardly amounts to a friendship is created through a remarkably brief series of encounters in which class distinctions dictate a debilitating absence of candour: Tom wary of appearing patronising, and Jim afraid of presumption; the result is that Tom becomes uncharacteristically brusque, and Jim grows more and more servile. The growth of the relationship is seen in an almost crepuscular light – 'moths were astir', 'a green liquid sky against which homing birds were black as ink'. The atmosphere of latency is enhanced by an abundance of natural sensations. The scents and sounds of the countryside are contrasted with the dinginess and roughness of the interior of Jim's kitchen at the climactic moment when Tom hands over the money, and they must part company. The air is thick with suppressed eroticism – so much so that no further description is necessary, an economy which is fully justified on artistic grounds, but which the author would probably have explained by saying that there was nothing further to describe.

3 The Necessity of Forrest Reid

Norman Vance

My mother knew Forrest Reid in the inter-war years. At least, they both lived in Ormiston Crescent in suburban east Belfast at that time, he at no.13 and she on the other side of the road at no.20. 'What was he like?' I once asked, only to be told that he was rather peculiar: friendly enough to the boys of the neighbourhood, but he definitely did not like little girls.

That sense of peculiarity and of remoteness from the full range of ordinary middle-class domestic life, involving little girls and their mothers as well as men and boys, is somehow characteristic. A strenuously literary education, eventually completed at Cambridge, had encouraged withdrawal into romantic reverie and the life of the imagination. He admired the early Yeats, and Yeats had seen himself as one of the last romantics, content to dream because 'in dreams begin responsibility'. Long and careful practice in the lonely craft of writing, as well as supportive contact with other writers such as Walter de la Mare and E. M. Forster, had gradually refined extreme sensitivity and a degree of shyness and social awkwardness into self-conscious aestheticism partly supported and expressed through select male friendships. This gave him the courage and the authority to stand a little apart, to privilege dream-consciousness over the world of action, to write the autobiographical *Apostate* and to develop apostasy into an art-form.

The Revd Dr Ian Paisley and the politicised would-be neo-Calvinist orthodoxies of his Free Presbyterian Church and Democratic Unionist Party flourished only after Reid's death in 1947, but 'apostasy' was and is one of Dr Paisley's favoured terms of theological abuse. Forrest Reid was an apostate from Paisley's Ulster even before Paisley: his specialised mode of life and feeling deplored but in a sense depended on a proto-Paisleyite mythologised Other represented by brutally censorious enemies of the free spirit and the literary imagination, in particular the unimaginative, commercially successful, dourly church-attending citizens of Belfast.

In revolting against this aspect of Belfast life Forrest Reid was repudiating aspects of his own family background. His father had once been a ship-owner though he had come down in the world to be a factory manager. His great-uncle, the Revd Professor James Seaton Reid, had been a distinguished nineteenth-century historian of Irish Presbyterianism who engaged in learned controversy with C. R. Elrington, the Anglican biographer of Archbishop Ussher – a controversy which had as much to do with the continuing political antagonism between Presbyterian dissenters and a privileged Anglican establishment as with the history of seventeenth-century Ireland. Forrest Reid chose to ignore politics and formal religion as much as possible and to write and think about other things.

This gently adversarial life as it was lived gave comfort and encouragement to the aspiring (male) writers of the city who came to know him and whose emerging sense of artistic identity required them, like him, to be or at least to feel alien and (probably) misunderstood in mercantile and industrial Belfast and in politically and religiously embattled Ulster. E. M. Forster's early tribute to Forrest Reid (1920), reprinted in *Abinger Harvest*, brilliantly and outrageously overstated the antagonism between provincial Belfast and the civilised imagination, as represented by Forrest Reid, offering a Dickensian caricature of the city distantly echoing the Coketown of *Hard Times*: 'Belfast, as all men of affairs know, stands no nonsense.' Forster recalled that the men of Belfast had almost overturned the car in which Mr Winston Churchill was travelling. He did not add that this was because of a certain patronising insensitivity on Churchill's part to local feeling on the vexed question of Home Rule, or appear to notice that his own aesthetic aloofness and disenchantment could be represented as an equally patronising variant of the same insensitivity and failure of moral sympathy.

Forster had a little self-consciously inherited the tastefully fashioned mantle of the intermittently insufferable Matthew Arnold, Victorian crusader against unalleviated 'Hebraism' – the narrow views, or at least the different views, of middle-class 'philistines', often more or less aggressively dissenters in religion. Such people could be represented, all too easily, as self-righteous, crassly materialistic and culturally impoverished, lacking a sense of beauty and a sense of proportion, insensitive to the enlarged imaginative possibilities bequeathed by the Greeks and summed up by Arnold as 'Hellenism'. It was not difficult for Forster to present mainly Protestant (and partly dissenting Presbyterian) Belfast, then in its economic heyday as a centre for ship-building, heavy engineering and textile manufacture, as a city of philistines. For would-be aesthetes who disliked Belfast politics, or at least the politics of Protestant unionism, Forster's version of Forrest Reid as the foe of the philistines, important in a way that they were not, helped to establish him as a valuable role-model for sensitive youths, and Reid had no difficulty in living up to the part.

But Reid's apostasy could be traced to much older sources independent of Forster's liberal humanism. Somewhere behind *Apostate* loomed the figure of Julian the Apostate, Roman Emperor, who had attempted to turn back the clock and restore the old paganism after Christianity had become the official religion of the Roman Empire under his immediate predecessor, Constantine. Nineteenth-century literary rebels such as the Norwegian dramatist Henrik Ibsen, admired by the young Forster, and the neo-pagan poet Algernon Swinburne had looked to Julian as a model, albeit an unsuccessful one, for their own modes of moral and social protest against their times. Literature, perhaps delicately and dangerously flavoured with classical paganism, had long been the aspiration and consolation of the suburban rebel or the post-Christian malcontent more interested in Pan or Plato than in prudery or commercial prudence. An early short story by E. M. Forster, 'The Story of a Panic', had fancifully brought Pan and happy paganism into direct and challenging confrontation with pious English philistinism. It was possible through literature and the imagination to enter into the liberating mind-set of other times and places, represented not just by writers but by painters and musicians. Forrest Reid came to admire the eighteenth-century French painter Watteau as the late-Victorian poet Austin Dobson had admired him, to respond to the Italian Renaissance painter Giorgione as the critic and aesthete Walter Pater had responded, to relish the exotically Romantic music of Berlioz and Wagner as the music-critic and dramatist George Bernard Shaw had done.

But it was particularly as an admirer of Greek paganism and as a translator from the Greek Anthology as well as in his quietly Greek admiration for youthful male beauty that Forrest Reid came to embody Hellenism, or Arnoldian sweetness and light, against the sturdier but more self-righteous Hebraism of Belfast linen-lordism and sectarian politics often buttressed with the less attractive features of Calvinism and intransigent religious dissent. Influential advocates of Greek culture such as Forster's friend Goldsworthy Lowes Dickinson, mentioned in Forster's letters to Reid, had tried to insist on the ethical as well as the aesthetic dimension of 'the Greek view of life' and to distinguish it from the self-consciously amoral aestheticism and decadence of the 1890s associated with Oscar Wilde. But Reid was unconvinced. For him, as for the French 'Parnassian' poet Leconte de Lisle in an earlier generation, the reimagined classical world provided a refuge for the beleaguered

values of art and beauty and refinement of feeling. In Milton's 'Nativity Ode', a favourite poem, the Christian poet had signalled the passing of Great Pan and paganism with the birth of Christ, but Reid chose to ignore the coming of Christ and developed a passion for Pan and for the Greek sense of divinity touching all natural things. Over the years he particularly treasured poems in the Greek Anthology which paid tribute to Pan and to unbaptised nature. He singled out lines attributed to Plato himself which invoke Pan playing on his sweet pipe, running his supple lips over the joined reeds while nymphs and nature-spirits join in the dance. He eventually compiled a volume of his translations, published in 1943.

Verse-translation from the classics had been the literary diversion of earlier generations, up to and including Mr Gladstone, but Forrest Reid's translations, modest, graceful and precise, were in prose. His prose renderings of short poems by Nikias or Euenos nestled naturally into the prose reveries of *Apostate*, completely assimilated to the non-Christian consciousness and spirituality of the writer. Earlier, often rather flat-footed and literal prose versions, such as those published in the Bohn or Loeb series, had provided a basis for his own work, but a distinctive tact and taste shines through in his improvements on them. Archaic 'thou' favoured by earlier translators becomes more modern 'you' without loss of dignity. 'Pretty' becomes less trivial as 'lovely'. The tired translator's cliché 'dust and ashes' in the Loeb version of a poem by Asklepiades becomes more literally and arrestingly 'bones and dust'. Greek word-order, particularly in poetry, is more flexible than English, so the rhetorical and poetic force of a particular verbal sequence is hard to preserve in translation, impossible in literal translation. But Reid often exercised considerable syntactic ingenuity, to good effect, in preserving the word order if not the strict grammatical form of his original.

Some of the epigrams of the Greek Anthology, which ranged over many centuries, were explicitly Christian, but Reid had no interest in them. The Greek word *hymnos* which occurred from time to time in the pagan poems was usually translated 'song' or 'air', but for Reid, translating Theokritos invoking the rustic flute-playing of fair-skinned Daphnis and offerings consecrated to Pan, the right word was 'hymn', both closer to the sound of the Greek and more precise in its separation of Christian content from ritual acts of celebration and homage to the world of nature and beauty.

Nietzsche's *Birth of Tragedy* had taught Reid's generation about the darker, Dionysiac aspect of the Greek reverence for nature, involving blood-sacrifice, lust and madness, but, like Arnold before him, Reid was not interested, was indeed repelled, distancing himself from such horror as 'the *truly* religious element, doubtless' of Greek culture. Like the black-coated religious dimension of Belfast life, this obtruded unpleasantly on the sunlit serenities of the imagination and was quickly banished.

In the increasingly depressing, troubled and poverty-stricken years between the wars it was necessary and important for Belfast youth to have access to the peace and freedom of the cultivated imagination. Through friendship and through his writing Forrest Reid helped at least a few to have that access. Great Pan was allowed to roam discreetly along Ormiston Crescent, even if my mother never had a chance to see him.

4 Brian Westby
John McGahern

Linton waits for the boy to join him in the car that is to take them to the boat, away from the mother. In its perfect description of suffering this strange, confused, sometimes brilliant and – I say it hesitatingly – seemingly dishonest work almost redeems itself:

It was twenty minutes to five, and Linton stood at the window looking out. He had paid his bill, his luggage had been brought downstairs, and the boots was now mounting guard over it in the hall. He had tipped the servants, had said good-bye to Miss O'Casey, had put on his coat, was ready to start. And suddenly he felt his whole body was shaking with nervous excitement.

This was stupid; he must control himself; there was no reason to be so agitated.

But the car was late . . . Well – no, it wasn't for he heard it at that moment at the door. Linton left the room and walked quickly down the passage.

His baggage was already being stowed away, and while this was proceeding he told the driver what he wanted him to do. He had told him before, but he told him again. He was the same man who had driven them to Fair Head and assured Linton that he understood: – they were to pick up the young gentleman – young Mr Westby – at the school . . . The boots was holding the door open, and Linton took his seat in the car.

Once they were started he felt better. It had been the interval between packing up and the arrival of the car which had proved so trying. He had found it impossible to do anything except watch the hands of the clock; but now, with the journey actually begun, though his excitement and anxiety had not decreased, he felt the relief that comes from action. He leaned back. Not looking out of the window, they drove past the post-office, past the turning down to the railway-station, past the shops in the main street, and on to the end of the town. There close to the side of the road and immediately opposite the school, the car drew up, and Linton looked out eagerly. But nobody was waiting.

Of course nobody *would* be waiting, he told himself: he was much too early. His hand was trembling as he unbuttoned his overcoat and fumbled for his watch, getting it out with some difficulty. Yes, he was eight minutes before his time. Once more he leaned back, and tried to drain his mind of all thought. He would not look out again until he heard footsteps. But almost immediately he did hear and started up.

It was only an old man carrying a spade over his shoulder. Linton leaned out of the window and gazed back along the straight dusty stretch of road. It was empty and bathed in sunlight. He sat now with his watch before him, his eyes fixed on the tiny hand that marked the seconds and was the only one which appeared to be moving. And then suddenly it seemed to be moving very fast indeed. And he watched it completing circle after circle. Somewhere behind him he heard a clock striking the hour, and directly afterwards the rumble and rattle of an approaching cart. The cart lumbered by. It was carrying a load of wet brown seaweed, and a man was walking at the horse's head, holding the bridle. Two girls passed on bicycles and after that nothing till a yellow cat appeared at the entrance of the school, pausing cautiously for a few seconds before gliding on round the side of the house . . . Linton put away his watch and shut his eyes . . . Brian was late . . .

A long time seemed to elapse before he felt a kind of faintness and struggled against it. He must not – he must not . . . Two or three drops of sweat trickled down his forehead. He took off his hat and wiped his forehead with his handkerchief . . .

The driver had got out some time ago. And now he approached Linton's door. 'How long am I to wait, sir?' he asked. 'It's nearly twenty-past.'

'How long *can* you wait?' Linton said, conscious that the man was looking at him strangely.

'Well – better not cut it *too* fine, sir. Say, a quarter to six at the latest.' But he still lingered by the door. And next moment he added awkwardly, 'What about getting out, sir, while we're waiting? You're looking kind of – not too well; and you'd maybe find it fresher outside. You could sit there on that wall.'

Linton followed his advice, though he did not sit down. He stood by the wall, resting his hand on it; and the driver stood by the door of the car and presently lit a cigarette. The clock chimed the half hour.

There was still plenty of time, Linton told himself. After all, even if they missed the boat –

Brian had said he would come by the inland road. Should he go back to meet him? It would be easier than waiting like this. But suppose he missed him! – suppose he came by another way! No, it would be safer to wait on here . . . Only, why didn't he come? Surely he must know that this kind of thing was an agony . . .

Again he shut his eyes, but opened them, almost at once, at the sound of an approaching car. It was climbing the long straight hill, and as it drew rapidly nearer both its shape and colour were vaguely familiar to Linton. 'Mr Graham's car, sir,' the driver mentioned as if reading his thought.

The car was almost abreast of them now. Now it *was* abreast: and now it had gone by – leaving a falling cloud of dust behind it. Linton stood gazing after it, though presently only at the empty road and through a kind of mist . . . What was he waiting for? There was no longer any need to wait. Yet still he stood there until the driver spoke.

'Wasn't the young gentleman in the car, sir?' he said, and Linton's lips moved though no sound issued from them.

'And he never looked out,' the driver muttered half to himself. 'The young lady – she looked out; but he kept *his* head down . . . Well, I suppose we needn't wait any longer.'

Linton took a step forward. 'No,' he said. 'We can go now.'

'You're not well, sir,' the man exclaimed, catching him by

the arm and speaking with a rough friendliness. 'If you ask me, I don't think you're fit for this drive. Best let me take you back to the hotel, and put it off till tomorrow.'

'Yes, I'll go back,' Linton murmured. 'Perhaps – tomorrow morning.'

He got into the car, stumbling clumsily over the step and the driver followed him. But while they were turning, Linton leaned forward. 'Take me to Mrs Belford's,' he said, 'not to the hotel.'

'All right, sir.' And they started.

At the post-office they branched off, going by the inland road, and when they stopped at Mrs Belford's door Linton got out. 'Perhaps you would take my things on to the hotel for me,' he said, 'and perhaps you would explain to them.'

'Hadn't I better wait for you, sir?' the man asked doubtfully.

'No thanks – I'll be all right now.' He stood motionless till the car had started: then he walked up to the house and knocked at the door.

Again it was Mrs Belford who answered it. Though this time she was prepared for visitors and immediately recognised Linton. 'They've gone, Mr Linton,' she said brightly: 'the whole family's gone. It's too bad you're missing them. For it's hardly a quarter of an hour since they left. With young Mr Graham who's going to drive them home.'

'Yes – I thought I saw them: I just wanted to know –'

Mrs Belford's face had suddenly altered: she was looking at him now the way the driver had looked. Why should they look at him like this? 'Mr Brian –' he said. 'I called in case he might have left a note for me – a message perhaps –'

He broke off as he saw there was no note, no message. Mrs Belford indeed seemed to have been struck dumb. But presently she answered, 'No, Mr Linton. No, he left no message.'

Linton felt himself flushing violently. 'Perhaps, at the hotel,' he stammered.

'Well, perhaps,' Mrs Belford agreed. But he could see, he could hear, that she was only trying to be kind and in fact almost immediately she contradicted herself. 'Mr Brian wasn't out all afternoon,' she said, 'and they didn't drive that way.' Next moment, however, she looked at him with increased uneasiness, as if conscious that for her hearer these words must hold some deeper and more painful significance than any she could find in them. 'Mr Brian wanted to,' she went on – 'he did his best to persuade them to go home by the coast, but Mr Graham had some reason for taking the back road, and the others wished to go that way too. I'm just telling you in case you'd be thinking maybe, they stopped to leave word for you in passing and be disappointed. It's more likely you'll get a letter in the morning.'

Linton said nothing; but neither did he move; and Mrs Belford, not caring to close the door while he still remained there, after waiting a little while was obliged to speak again. 'Mrs Westby didn't make up her mind to go until two o'clock. Both she and Mr Brian seemed very much upset, and though she didn't say so, I'm sure something unexpected must have happened. She only told me it would be necessary for them to get home to-day. Maybe it was young Mr Graham who brought a message, for he was the only one that called. And I know there was no telegrams or letters. It was decided all in a hurry, you might say; and I don't think they can have been expecting you.'

'Thank you,' Linton murmured.

The sun was hurting his eyes, and he pulled his hat lower. For a few seconds he shut his eyes. It was this glare, this heat . . . Then he turned again to the house but Mrs Belford was gone and the door closed: the house itself, in fact, was several yards away. He didn't remember her shutting the door . . .

Perhaps – anyhow he must not stand here, and he began to descend the hill.

When he reached the hotel he turned to the left and went down to the shore. He found the place where they had sat that morning making their plans. But the tide was farther out now: there was a broad strip of uncovered yellow sand between the rocks and the sea.

It is as beautifully calm as Henry James's, one of Forrest Reid's masters, ending of *Washington Square*: 'Catherine, meanwhile in the parlour, picking up her morsel of fancywork had seated herself with it again – for life, as it were.'

It has, above all, which Reid always has, often when not even writing well, the same gloved sureness and mastery of prose rhythm. I print it in full, not only for its beauty, but because it is not in print and should be. It is, perhaps, the finest single chapter Reid ever wrote.

The plot is improbable enough, Reid choosing to limp along with the conventions that he is plainly unhappy in. Linton has had a near-fatal illness. When his doctor suggested somewhere quiet by the sea to complete the recovery, Ballycastle was instantly in his mind like a vision, and he yielded to it and came – although he had hardly thought of the place more than twice since he'd last visited it more than twenty years before. As for Stella, with whom he had first visited the place, he had not heard of her since their separation and divorce, other than that she had wanted the divorce to marry Westby; and he had no reason to believe he was less or more likely to meet her in Ballycastle than anywhere else. He has just come to this quiet place by the sea to complete his recovery, and not to write, – but the trouble is that with the drying up of his creative faculty he has nothing to live for.

As he strolls across the golf links on his first morning in Ballycastle, he feels his life has failed, and he sees where it has failed:

Happiness is only made by affection. Nothing else in the long run matters. The responsibilities and anxieties that accompany affection are in themselves blessings. He had no responsibilities, no anxieties, and he felt that he had lived long enough.

Yet he feels beauty endlessly flow by him, but he is powerless to arrest it, through some moral or spiritual disintegration: *'For there is no such thing as beauty without a human interpretation of it.'* Then he comes on the boy, and recognises his own first novel by its cover on the dry grass beside him. Linton pauses as the boy looks briefly up, but, as he does not look up again, after a moment's hesitation he passes on. But his whole mood has dramatically changed. Everything seems closer to him, acquires a new value. 'The whole scene had acquired an interest.'

On his way back he engages the boy in conversation about his own first novel, pretending to be a friend of Linton. This arouses the boy's curiosity as to what sort of person Linton is. This, in turn, leads to a discussion about writing in general, and to the boy's confession that he is engaged in writing a novel. As he listens to the boy's description of what he is writing, Linton realises with dismay, for already he is extraordinarily attracted to the boy – Brian Westby – that it is unlikely to be his kind of novel: but finds consolation in the knowledge 'that if there is one quality the writings of the young rarely or never reflect, it is the spirit of youth, Brian's very attraction for him; and anyhow he regards precocity as being of all the qualities the least promising'. They part after Brian promises to bring Linton part of his novel to read.

In alternating chapters, through Brian's eyes and then Linton's, the scene unfolds, Jamesian lamps playing on the dark central object. It is even coyly played with:

'Don't you think the weather might account for it?' Linton said. 'The sunshine – or possibly the view? The view, as a matter of fact, I'm sure had something to do with it.'
    'What view?'
    '*My* view . . . You needn't look,' he went on: 'you won't be able to see it, because you're part of it . . .'

There is play, too, throughout the whole work on the words *interest* and *sympathy*, without which Life or Beauty hardly live at all; and they both serve to illumine and veil the paedophilic nature of Linton's love, as the superficial plot probably reveals that the boy isn't Brian Westby but Brian Linton, Linton's own son, and that he is here for the season in Ballycastle with his mother and half-sister. An accident has conveniently kept the mother indoors until now. For a time, and especially since this first part is prefaced by, 'As in water face answereth to face, so the heart of man to man,' it appears that Reid may be using the plot's device to have the writer at the end of his career meet with himself when he was taking the first crude steps in his art; to have set, in fact, his drama firmly in the well of Narcissus. Here, it has some affinity with Hardy's *The Well-Beloved*, and this current does flow among the other confused currents throughout most of the work.

In *The Day-Spring*, the novel's second part rung in by Wordsworth's 'Our souls have sight of that immortal sea', Linton's sense of Stella's perfidy in concealing his son's existence from him at their separation and divorce justifies him in continuing to conceal his own true identity. Time had meant everything to him – time which had permitted the boy to get to know him, to get to like him, to form his own impression of him. As in the first part, when the sight of Brian drew him closer to the whole natural scenery, he now determines to use the time to draw closer to the essential in the boy's personality, to reach past his changing or hostile moods, to what Linton feels to be constant 'when he is responsive, affectionate, sympathetic . . .' The boy now becomes an echo of the artist's traditional relationship with the Muse:

Moreover, he was not only aware of this spirit intellectually, he could actually see it – see it clearly as he could see the boy's body. And he had a feeling that if he should ever really offend or distress it he would never see it again.

At Linton's suggestion, they begin to collaborate on a story. There is much talk of writing. Reid, through Linton's words, states his own true vision of the activity:

It's true, Brian, you know, you *can* have such a vision: – something which remains ever afterwards as an influence – which creates an ideal – and a longing that it may come again . . . You don't want to write the kind of stuff which can't be read a second time until the first reading is forgotten – which depends on mere surprise for its interest. There must be something behind – or rather all through your work – a spiritual atmosphere. It seems to me that this alone can give it richness. Art isn't just life in the raw: it is a selection from life: it *is* a vision: life seen through a temperament, as Bola said. And its quality depends on the quality of that temperament far more than on the material out of which the actual pattern is woven.

But it is here, in this literary hothouse, that the novel is at its worst: Winter coyly hiding its desire for Spring's young body beneath the cloak of Instruction. Side by side with this 'spiritual drawing closer' the 'plot' is pushed uncertainly along. So much artificiality and subterfuge have had to be resorted to that when the prose reaches for what only has interested it from the beginning of *The Day-Spring*, the revelation of the eternal or spiritual in the mortal – beautiful as it is in itself – has, because of the insincerity and pure embarrassment of much that has led up to it, been drained of much of its credibility. It is as if Proust, while gazing on the sleeping Albertine, should be writing of the death of Bergotte:

The accumulated affection of years had found at last an outlet, and in this passion of protective tenderness which filled him, his life acquired a new meaning and usefulness. Had there not been, in the very fact of their meeting, something which suggested intention, beneficence, a conscious providence? It so easily might not have happened, and that it should have happened made so wonderful a difference! Surely if there were any spiritual reality at all, an emotion which aroused and encouraged all that was best and least selfish in him could not be wasted? And it would be wasted if, to the object of it, it might as well never have been; if it awakened no response, if it did no good, if it lived and died only in itself. For it was primarily an impulse to give, an impulse to share – not only material things, but the beauty of this summer day for instance – the beauty that has been achieved by the spirit and genius of mankind working on, age by age, in poetry and stone and music – the beauty that is goodness. And it was an impulse to protect – to protect from what is hurtful and evil. And it was an impulse to strengthen and encourage and arm, to implant wisdom and independence, to quicken generosity, admiration and compassion . . .

The Choice, the third and final part, is prefaced again by Wordsworth's lines from one of the late sonnets:

Speak! – though this soft warm heart, once free to hold
A thousand tender pleasures, thine and mine,
Be left more desolate, more dreary cold
Than a forsaken bird's nest . . .
Speak, that my torturing doubts their end may know!

Early in this part the work begins to recover much of its dignity. Yet, since Linton cannot be seen to be conscious of his true feelings, a degree of tact and maturity is thrust on the boy that his character can hardly credibly support. But when Linton discloses his true identity to the boy on Fair Head, it is with almost physical relief that the prose casts off its dependence on the conventions. (In the light of Stanislaus Joyce's statement on the different position compared to his English counterpart the Irish writer's lack of a tradition immediately places him in, it is interesting that the attempt of Forrest Reid's friend, E. M. Forster, to write outside the conventions in *Maurice* was to prove at least as disastrous as Reid's inability to dispense with them in *Brian Westby*.)

Now that Linton is declared the boy's father, there is no longer need of deceit and subterfuge. It is ironic that one of Linton's first criticisms of his own early work should be: 'In fact it's worse than feeble, it's insincere; and I hate insincerity. I hate it in life: and in art, of course, it's fatal.' Freed finally of the need of insincerity by declaring himself openly the boy's father, Linton's guilty love is legitimised. Clear as the words of Wordsworth the prose rings out that it is speaking of what Proust calls that carnal attraction of any profundity, carrying always within it the possibility of calamity, that men call love:

Presently he was sure it was; and as he sat there, he saw his dream fading, dying. And a grey desolation stretching out in its place. The sudden collapse of what had been more than hope brought with it a kind of physical sickness. As if all that was vital in him had been drained away, leaving a feeling of emptiness, weakness. And exhaustion. 'I'm sorry,' he muttered.

The prose can now cry out in the naked language of love:

It was as instinctive in a human soul to reach after happiness as it was in a plant to turn to the sun, and it would be the veriest hypocrisy to pretend that the knowledge that Brian was happy would in itself be sufficient, should he never see him again, to make *him* happy. It wouldn't. Nor could he now, he thought, find courage to face the existence which had been tolerable a few weeks ago, because, even to reach *that* apathetic state he would first have to become indifferent, have to forget. And in a sudden final flash of self-knowledge he spoke aloud the truth: 'I cannot live without him.'

I cannot live without him. The heart is caged:

Then the question would come – half shyly, half confidently – 'When do you want me again?' It was extraordinary how those simple words could give him so much pleasure – so much pleasure at the time, so much pleasure afterwards in recollection. A word, an intonation, a passing change of expression, a sudden smile – what was there in things like these which seemed to twine them around one's very heart so that never afterwards could they be forgotten?

As Linton stands unaware of the rain, devouring the sight of the boy in the lighted room, and, as the light suddenly goes out, there is the premonition of disaster:

Suddenly, without even a warning flicker, the light upon which Linton's eyes were fixed went out, and he found himself alone in the darkness. So abruptly it happened that he had the sense of a physical shock, violent and brutal. Instantly the empty dreary night was there. And he became conscious of the rain and the cold – and of his own body chilled and cramped and wet, while far down below on the desolate shore at the cliff's edge, he heard the remote unresting crying of the sea. Yet the shock was less physical than spiritual. It was like a callous and cruel awakening. Until now, through all his long vigil, he had had the feeling that Brian was with him. The river of light flowing between them had been a bond. Now this bond was broken, and in the darkness Linton knew he was alone. And his loneliness aroused in him an intense desire to attract the boy's attention – to call to him, to throw a handful of gravel at his window – a desire none the less acute because he never for a moment dreamed of yielding to it.

Brian gravely counterpoints it:

As for himself, happiness – lasting happiness – he thought, was impossible. He didn't feel that there was anything to be happy about – either in the past, the present or the future. You were happy in the beginning perhaps, as a puppy or a kitten is happy – but once that brief period was ended, once you came in contact with the reality and began to, think the world grew steadily darker . . . He remembered a remark Mr Martin had once made, that life, even at its worst, will always seem to be worth living if there is somebody for whom you care sufficiently. Some one or some thing . . . But supposing there wasn't? All that remained then was the feeling that there are certain duties which you must do your best to fulfil, though even where *that* feeling came from, or why you had it, you did not know. Only there was nothing else – and the sooner you had done your task the better.

The struggle with the mother for the boy's affection is no longer caught in the toils of the plot, has only superficial relevance, as love's sickness feeds on poisonous hope.

It took shape and colour in his imagination – a dream of renewed life and happiness. It grew brighter and brighter, more and more tempting – a dream of their life together – of work and of leisure, of sympathy and friendship, of shared thoughts and feelings and plans, of the long intimacy of firelit winter evenings, of summer holiday, of watching Brian's career, of helping in it, of being present when he had his first success. The dream rose before his inward gaze, like a summer-morning sun over a lonely world, filling the sky and drenching the earth with its light and warmth and blessing. And from a dream it could so easily pass to reality! There could be plenty of time later to discuss details – to plan and to settle. Plenty of time – an enchanted river cool and fresh and clear, flowing on and on to an unknown sea . . .

But in the last perfect chapter about suffering Forrest Reid was not wrong:

But the tide was farther out now: there was a broad strip of uncovered yellow sand between the rocks and the sea.

I think of two other works alongside *Brian Westby*. They are far more truly realised and both German: Mann's *Death in Venice* and Hesse's *Damian*. They are both romantic and written within an established tradition. This Forrest Reid did not have. Linton seems to realise that he has hardly the means to be a novelist at all:

I mean, he's got an ideal; and each of his books is an attempt to express it. So far as it *is* his book, that, is to say, for the subject sometimes won't allow it to be. That's what I meant when I said he chose the wrong subject. There's only the faintest glimmer of what he's really after in op.one, for instance; and in none even of his latest books, perhaps, is it there all the time.

Yet, Forrest Reid has what is more in this ideal never far and never lost in the beautiful rhythmical prose, a true and permanent voice. And for all its flaws as a work, this voice rings out more powerfully and poignantly in parts of *Brian Westby* than perhaps anywhere else in Reid's many books.

There is a letter of Proust's, where he protests at the exclusion of the village curé from the school committee, saying that he should be there with the tobacconist and newsagent and tax collector if for nothing else but the spire of his church, which lifts men's eyes from the avaricious earth. Such a spire is still at the heart of *Brian Westby* and all Reid's work. That spire is but a symbol of what Reid himself has beautifully called a moral fragrance.

Rich as his best work is in its echoes of great pastoral poetry, as well as the prose rhythms of Henry James and Jane Austen in the delicate sense of timing, the voice might never have become individual without the tension of being Irish, of being outside the tradition he knew and loved: and he might have become just another English writer of no very great distinction. Or, freed of the tension by being born within the tradition, his work might have been more fully realised, less warped. We cannot know. What we do know, a hundred years after his birth, is that he has a firm place, private and a little apart, in a younger tradition, and he is as necessary there as Proust's curé should have been if for nothing else but that he wrote uncommonly well.

5   Child's-eye View: the Autobiographies of Forrest Reid

Angela Thirlwell

To write one autobiography is risky. To follow it with a sequel could be sheer folly. But this is exactly what Forrest Reid did, publishing *Apostate* in 1926 and *Private Road* in 1940.

He wrote *Apostate* in the eighteen months leading up to his fiftieth birthday, a year of emergency in most people's lives, a year that naturally invites stocktaking and the daring enterprise of autobiography. Benvenuto Cellini [1] thought that everyone who cared for truth ought to turn to this task in exactly these middle years. Mid-life is a crisis, as Doris Lessing notes: 'Somewhere about middle age, it occurs to most people that a century is only their own lifetime twice. On that thought, all of history rushes together, and now they live inside the story of time, instead of looking at it from outside, as observers.' [2] Fifty is a watershed; fifty is a spur to the writers of autobiography. Cellini and Lessing [3] are both memorable autobiographers but Reid stands apart from them, and indeed from nearly all other autobiographers in the Western tradition.

Of course, many autobiographers deal with childhood and adolescence, usually in ther opening chapters; some like Eric Gill, [4] Georgia O'Keefe [5] and Jean-Paul Sartre [6] write on their early years magically, indelibly, furiously. Very few choose to focus entirely on life's earliest experiences like Reid in *Apostate*, his first autobiography, although others who did include Walter Pater, [7] Gwen Raverat [8] and Laurie Lee. [9] More recently, Janet Frame, [10] Christy Nolan [11] and Seamus Deane [12] have sent back first-hand despatches from the front of childhood. How, then, from so much autobiographical treasure, does Reid's *Apostate* stand out and command a special hearing?

I think it is because this short, unpretentious volume has such authenticity. In 1918 W. H. Hudson called his boyhood *Far Away and Long Ago*, but it was near at hand for Reid: the past thrillingly informed the present at every turn. As a middle-aged adult, Reid still convinces us that he can think and feel as a child. His joys and disenchantments, his aspirations and embarrassments are conveyed to the reader in another time, another place, with vivid intensity. His dreams are still tangible; from them he can recover remembered moments of childhood that the reader is able to share and recognise. In addition, as novelist and critic, Reid understands the crucial imperative of selection, using artifice to appear natural.

Looking back from *Private Road*, he claimed that perhaps, 'of all my books' *Apostate* 'was the easiest to write' because he had 'nothing to change, nothing to invent, nothing to ponder. I simply watched and listened, while the whole thing was re-enacted before me.' The writer and the boy fuse to produce a child's-eye view that transports the adult reader. With considerable self-knowledge, Reid identified the sources of his art 'in emotion, intuition, vision, a soil lying below the intellect, and deeper, darker, and richer than it'. The act of autobiography can be viewed as a prodigious act of narcissism. Yet the strength of Reid's autobiographies, and of his novels, derives from his commitment to that self. 'I aimed at nothing except the expression of my individual sense of life', which is neither a boast nor an admission but quite simply the task that the best autobiographers must set themselves.

As titles *Apostate* and *Private Road* seem curious, contradictory choices at first glance. *Apostate* is bold, iconoclastic, arresting. *Private Road* is both reclusive and exclusive, even self-effacing. Reid was well aware of the importance of titles and tried out different titles for his fiction. He was equally thoughtful about his autobiographical titles. 'Other people, it is true, for some unknown reason preferred to call it *The Apostate*, but that falsified my meaning, the title was intended to indicate a state of mind, not a person . . .' Omitting the definite article loaded *Apostate* with dramatic force and symbolic freight.

The title *Private Road* is less immediately striking than *Apostate* but its quiet allusiveness gathers significance. 'Looking back through Time' (early in *Apostate*) Reid 'cannot help thinking that I was in those days very much what I am now. My life, from as far back as I can remember, was never lived wholly in the open. I mean that it had its private side, that there were things I saw, felt, heard, and kept to myself.' The private road, like the private side of life, is both inviting and debarring at the same time. The balance between revelation and reticence in autobiography gives us key information about the personality. 'Kiss and tell' may be the slogan of a brasher age but Reid's subtler art lay in 'dream and show'. The reader may hear other echoes in *Private Road*, perhaps of Yeats's line 'He made the world to be a grassy road', quoted by Reid. The image of a road is a widely used metaphor for life itself; countless children have learnt by rote Christina Rossetti's insistent question: 'Does the road wind up-hill all the way?'

In tenor if not as titles, *Apostate* and *Private Road* stand in relation to one another rather like Blake's *Songs of Innocence* to his *Songs of Experience*. Of course 'innocence' is touched by experience even in *Apostate* and 'experience' can be irradiated by innocence in the later volume. Autobiography as a genre is equally complex. It is both a demanding literary task and a daring personal exercise involving truth, lies and self-justification. Autobiography that focuses on childhood is doubly deceptive. The fallibility, the suggestibility of memory raises crucial problems for both writers and readers of childhood autobiographies. How much can we trust the writer? How far is the imaginative fleshing-out of a dimly remembered world permissible? Should we as readers collude in the pretence that this is really what it felt like to be that child, in that time and place? After all, it is an adult, and indeed a middle-aged adult in Reid's case, who is recreating a long past childhood. Inevitably, the autobiography must tell us more about the adult who is now writing than the child that writer once was. The action of Time must distort the truth in spite of Reid's best intentions. 'Time, I find, has dropped veil beyond veil between me and the real world I am trying to evoke. I may promise to present it . . . without a rag of disguise, but I know I cannot keep my promise' (*Apostate*). He emphasised the patchiness of memory by choosing to quote from Max Beerbohm in one of four epigraphs to *Private Road*: 'Elderly persons would be utterly intolerable if they remembered *everything*. *Everything*, nevertheless, is just what they themselves would like to remember, and just what they would like to tell to *everybody*. Be sure that the Ancient Mariner, though he remembered quite as much as his audience wanted to hear, and rather more, about the albatross and the ghastly crew, was inwardly raging at the sketchiness of his own mind.'

In spite of his self-doubt, Reid manages to overcome the sketchiness, to select from the selective nature of memory itself, its most intense and indelible experiences. For Reid his past childhood was more accessible than it is for most writers, for most people perhaps. For him the past was a vast and immediate resource. He sensed the past imminent in the present, palpably part of the world around him 'like the droning of bees' (*Private Road*). His recurring theme throughout both these autobiographies is the creative interaction between boy past and man and writer present. 'I cannot help thinking that I was in those days very much what I am now' (*Apostate*). The child is father of this man. Childhood was his fate, his chosen subject, and he re-examined it continually through adult eyes miraculously unmisted by the cataracts of Time.

However, writers may tell more autobiographical truth in fiction than in the genre of autobiography itself. Nowhere is adolescence more powerfully reassembled than in autobiographical novels such as D. H. Lawrence's *Sons and Lovers* (1913), James Joyce's *Portrait of the Artist as a Young Man* (1914/15), and Jeanette Winterson's *Oranges are not the only fruit* (1985). Reid acknowledges that the autobiographical impulse inspires some of his finest novels. He doesn't merely identify with Tom in *Uncle Stephen* (1931) but asserts that 'I undoubtedly was Tom' (*Private Road*). Reid reached back through veil upon veil of the years to recapture his own lost boyhood in the literary re-creation of Tom, a phantom so real that 'I knew the tones of his voice, I caught glimpses of him in the street, and one evening, after finishing a chapter, I put down my work to go out for a walk with him' (*Private Road*).

If the fictional Tom was 'absolutely real', he was so with an overlay of Vaughan-like luminescence, a very special little boy who 'felt through all this earthly dress bright shoots of everlastingness' (*Private Road*). The 'real' little boy of *Apostate* is the source material for the fictional Tom. Out of the life came the art, and creativity was the consolation for a lost childhood.

Reid's two autobiographies, separated by the differing perspectives of age fifty and age sixty-five, are very different in their structure and methods of telling. Although there is an underlying chronological narrative thrust, *Apostate* proceeds thematically, using a 'spots of time' approach reminiscent of Wordsworth's *Prelude* (1805) or Shen Fu's *Six Records of a Floating Life* written in China in 1809. From the selection of memory itself, Reid made further selections so that chapters seem to flow effortlessly from one another. He alternates external characters and events, Emma, Professor Park, sisters, friends, Belfast, adventures and hobbies, with abstract themes such as the self, religion, dreamland, poetry and the origins of creativity.

The chapter which gives *Apostate* its title deals with Reid's adolescent un-conversion, away from Christianity towards a personalised version of ancient Greek religion, closely allied to Wordsworth's pantheism. This chapter is artfully placed at the climax, or 'false end' of the autobiography, number nineteen out of a total of twenty-two. The dramatic and visionary nature of Chapter XIX is wryly counterpointed with the bathos of the chapter which immediately follows it on his early apprenticeship to the tea-trade and a botched suicide attempt. The young Reid recovers, first through a programme of self-education and then in the dazzling prospect of first love, to reach a second climax at the end of the book. The diminuendo of disappointment that concludes *Apostate* is moving and recognisable to all who recall the agonies of adolescence.

Private Road is often compared unfavourably with *Apostate*. It has struck commentators as somehow less endearing, as an adult seems in comparison with a child. But the structure of this second autobiography, nearly fifteen years after the first, is quietly daring. Although a linear, chronological structure underlies the narrative, *Private Road* is richly textured almost like a collage, incorporating complete or partial letters from friends and celebrities (such as Henry James, Padraic Colum, Edmund Gosse and Basil de Selincourt) as well as poetry, reviews, anecdotes, quotations, dialogue, literary criticism, pen portraits and extracts from his own early writer's notebook. The penultimate chapter departs from prose altogether and is a poem, 'The Pear Tree', that visually embodies the essence of Reid's theme. His boyhood self is mischievously shaking the boughs of the pear tree, an image powerfully reminiscent of the young St Augustine (the first autobiographer of a conversion story in the Western tradition) who remembered that 'close to our vineyard there was a pear tree, heavy with fruit' and how 'I and a group of wanton boys went to shake and steal the fruit from the tree'. Reid's image of his pear tree stretches back to St Augustine's boyish prank and resonates with that first innocence of a tree and a boy in the Garden of Paradise:

> And you look down at me, laughing and calling
>   through the green leaves.

Reid's pear tree 'All stripped of its fruit is now silent and naked' and symbolises experience and ageing too. In spite of this bleak realisation, the pear tree blossoms internally like his boyhood:

> My pear tree is growing within me: its branches are green.
> You shake it and call, 'How many? One fell close by Roger'.*
> And Roger will wait and you laugh and look down through the
>   branches
> For ever and ever.

This chapter as poem with its natural, rooted, central image is as unforgettable as St Augustine's pear tree or Katherine Mansfield's complex, concluding symbol in *Bliss*: 'But the pear tree was as lovely as ever and as full of flower and as still.'[13]

The chapters of *Private Road* are as skilfully counterpointed as those in *Apostate*. For example, the end of the fourth chapter is left dramatically poised awaiting the reaction of Henry James to Reid's novel *The Garden God* (1905) which he had fatefully dedicated to the great novelist: 'in the meantime I had heard from the Master at Lamb House, Rye'. The opening of the following chapter ironically picks up the last sentence: 'And the Master was not pleased'. The self-mockery of the simple syllables with their reverse Biblical echoes is a portent of the bitterest literary blow of Forrest Reid's career.

Private Road presented quite different problems for Reid from *Apostate* which he had been able to write 'just as it happened'. Later 'in the swarming years that followed I could discern no pattern'. When the mainspring of life may come unsprung, its purposes seem random or inexplicable, the autobiographer hopes to uncover patterns that help to order or explain life's haphazard batterings. 'The following of such thematic designs

through one's life should be, I think, the true purpose of autobiography', considered Vladimir Nabokov in *Speak, Memory*.[14] If Reid could discover no pattern, his way ahead in *Private Road* was bound to be less foot-sure than in *Apostate*. So his main purpose – to examine the development of his creative self – is augmented in the later book with memoir and anecdote, less intensely re-imagined than the driving ego of boyhood in *Apostate*. *Private Road* was diluted, as sequels often are. *Apostate* had been necessary to his spirit, a book he had loved writing and which had been well received. 'Could I carry it further?' he wondered and some critics have thought not. But although more diffuse and less obviously focused than *Apostate*, the later autobiography has different rewards for anyone who relishes the wide-ranging possibilities of autobiographical writing.

Private Road is comforting for those of us who have to grow up. In its pages, childhood is less retrievable than in *Apostate*. There the child who 'wanted to be a boy always' carries total conviction. The reader is implicated in the writer's pact with Time and believes with Reid not only that 'the years of childhood, boyhood, and adolescence are the most significant', but that we are inside the imagination of the writer's childhood self.

To take boyhood as the major theme of autobiography necessarily implies Time as its corollary. Time brings losses, the loss of that childhood and the loss of love that is implicit even in the finding of love. As the Australian poet Les Murray accurately notes: 'As usual after any triumph, I was of course inconsolable'.[15] Forrest Reid was inconsolable for the loss of his childhood and his solution was to re-invent it, reorder it and relive it through the patterns of art both in fiction and in autobiography.

Some autobiographers have idealised their early childhood in the altering light of memory, for example William Wordsworth, Rabindranath Tagore,[16] and Eva Hoffman.[17] Others have felt compelled to go back down the corridor of years to fill with incandescence a childhood that was clearly, ironically, less than perfect. Reid perceived his mother as coldly unloving; his father died when he was about five; his fatherlessness may have fed into his other feelings of loss. In adulthood, his paternal feelings for young boys may have been linked not only with his love and longing for his own lost boyhood self but also with the absence of a father in his growing-up days. The ghostly little boy he glimpses on a hotel landing is not just representative of all the boys he has loved – 'I saw that little boy, pursued him, and lost him' – but also a vision of his own lost child self. 'I never saw my little boy again' – Forrest Reid's personal tragedy in just ten syllables.

Autobiographers often elevate a vision of childhood that was far from perfect at the time by setting it in relation to later unhappiness or loss. Like Reid, Nabokov achingly evokes a 'sense of security, of well-being, of summer warmth. That robust reality makes a ghost of the

---

* Roger was a sheepdog

present. Everything is as it should be, nothing will ever change, nobody will ever die.' Nabokov's feelings about childhood are significantly associated with a life before exile from his native Russia.

Exile is a key component, too, in Reid's feelings for his past self. As an adult, he is in exile from the imagined Eden of his childhood, no less tangible for him than Russia was for Nabokov, or Poland for Eva Hoffman. Reid was an internal exile; as the youngest child within his crowded family, he felt constantly excluded from the superior secrets of his older siblings. By the time he was seventeen, he felt isolated too from his old street friends who now ran after girls. In the months of depression between leaving school and starting in the tea-trade 'I became obsessed that I was different from everybody else'. His teenage sense of being somehow outside acceptable society, metaphorically 'outside the pale', is reminiscent of Anthony Trollope who wrote, 'I felt myself to be a kind of pariah', in his autobiography, published posthumously in 1883. Reid's recompense for his sense of exile, for being an outsider, was that these negative, de-stabilising feelings became the sources of his positive, creative life as a writer. Only in writing could he recapture that inner, other, dream-life of his childhood, 'that lost green island of the earlier years, which I could no longer visit in the old way'. Conversely, only in revisiting the past could he become a fully creative artist.

I think it may well be true to say that the dream-life of childhood is more acutely remembered and rendered by Forrest Reid than by any other autobiographer I have read. His boyhood dream-world is still tantalisingly close to him even in adulthood, 'an enchanted land . . . in the rich deep drowsy' afternoons, of summer seas, remote mountains, smooth green lawns, foam and music. His favourite dream 'was pure happiness . . . always summer, always a little after noon, and always the sun was shining. The place was a kind of garden.' This dream landscape of almost unspeakable beauty was Reid's private antidote to isolation and exile. 'I did not feel lonely . . . I was happy . . . I had a sense of security . . . It was as if I had come home.' Because of the intensity, the sheer vividness of this dreamland, this 'remote Atlantis' seemed more real than the reality of everyday life which paled in the comparison: 'my waking life only partially satisfied me'. In Reid's fictional trilogy, the boy Tom retrieved from dreamland has a special nimbus around him reflecting 'the glory and the freshness of a dream'.

The longed-for inhabitant of this world of dreams is, of course, an ideal dream companion, recalling the first love of autobiographer Alexander Herzen whom he had loved 'long and passionately before I dared to call him "friend" . . . He was the first to use "thou" in writing to me; and he called me Damon before I called him Pythias. Smile, if you please, but let it be a kindly smile, such as men smile when recalling their own fifteenth year. Perhaps it would be better to ask, "Was *I* like that in my prime?"

and to thank your stars, if you ever *had* a prime, and to thank them doubly, if you had a friend to share it.'[18] The ideal dream companion for Reid is the perfect listener, perhaps his ideal reader. So when he attempts to merge the friend of his fantasies with a real, living, breathing boy contemporary there is bound to be disappointment. Reid offers his diary to Andrew Rutherford. It is an initiation into Reid's most secret world as well as a tacit avowal of his feelings. No real companion could compete with the dream companion. As Andrew reads the diary, *Apostate* fittingly ends on the tension of his silence, 'so intense that I felt nothing could ever again break it'.

Resuming his dream-life offered powerful compensation after the emotional drift apart from Andrew Rutherford. Once before, Reid had hoped to mesh the real world with his inner dream-world, when he had come under the spell of Alan Cunningham, a boy of insouciance and criminal potential, who nevertheless inspired Reid with 'sadness and rapture', and a sense of 'almost intolerable beauty'. After the excitement of two toughies housebreaking together, Reid finally realises that Alan is a long way from being a dream playmate. On the contrary, Alan had led him into a world of disenchantment, everything was unforgivably altered between them and 'I saw things exactly as they were'.

His ideal of perfect communion with another human being, a dream boy in a dream landscape, naked, pale amber, always about his own age, may have been an expression both of ineffable yearning for the Other and unbearable yearning for his own self, made Other by time. Or, as Donne's Sappho says, 'restore/Me to me; thee, my half, my all, my more.'[19] Self and the Other overlap, as the past spills into the present, as the dream-world melts into reality, each state vivid and absorbing.

With such heightened sensibilities, it is almost surprising that there are not more rapturous, epiphanic moments throughout Reid's autobiographies. Too many would have diluted their power, for when they do come they lift the reader, as in this ecstatic apprehension of the natural world in springtime: 'piercing up through the brown earth, breaking into flower – breaking into a flame of intense blue that burned and blazed and splashed all over the lush green of the deeper hollows. I drew the air far down into my lungs and raised my voice in my own kind of hymn.'

This euphoric response both to Mother Nature and, by implication, to his own human, sexual nature is in direct line of descent from Thomas Traherne,[20] Richard Jefferies,[21] and Walter Pater's cult of intense experience.[22] But Reid's epiphanies, like love itself, had a negative edge. During a misty moonlit night on a seaside holiday, the young Reid glimpsed the line of the bay and the unearthly, enchanted forms of naked bathers around it. The scene was like a painting of ethereal loveliness, although no painting could do justice to its beauty, 'a kind of spiritual loveliness'. Beauty inevitably brought the eternal note of sadness in and awoke 'that old endless home-sickness, that old longing for a heaven that was not heaven, for an earth that was not earth, for a love that I knew I should never find either in heaven or on earth'.

The natural beauties of seascape and landscape represented deeper, even moral beauties. Lovely landscapes of the mind, especially of childhood, were paralleled in the external world. Outer landscape linked to inner mood inspired his personal religion. He was moved equally by elemental images, the 'glory of sunset glistening on the sea below me', as well as by nature's smallest details, lavender, cotoneaster, barberry, the leaves of waterlilies, frogs or a crimson spotted ladybird.

For Western autobiographers, St Augustine's *Confessions* (AD 397) is the prototype autobiography. In it Augustine examines the dynamics of his personal conversion story from depravity to repentance, from paganism to Christianity. Since then, some of the most powerful autobiographies have turned on moments of conversion or, more sensationally, of un-conversion from belief to unbelief. Both of these contrasting auto-biographical impulses have their roots in the confessional. The losing of faith has been movingly documented by autobiographers and novelists as diverse as Charles Darwin,[23] Annie Besant,[24] Edmund Gosse,[25] Jean-Paul Sartre and Jeanette Winterson.[26] *Apostate* stands with these personal accounts and is equally unforgettable. On the day set for his confirmation into the Church of Ireland, Reid noted ironically that 'what had been designed as the beginning of my religious life proved to be the end of it'. He was sick of slavery to 'empty conventions' and radically, 'on the very next Sunday I refused point-blank to go to church any more'.

Un-converted from Christianity at the very moment of his confirmation, Reid 'confirmed' himself into a private religion that animated his whole being with the philosophy of Socrates rather than St Paul. Increasingly he was drawn into a personal view of the divine. 'Man has made God – many Gods indeed – in his own image'. Inspired by the Socratic ideal of loving the good, he adopted a deeply personal version of a Greek world-view with its sense of the divine in nature, its genius for friendship and its sense of eternal youth: 'the beauty of the earth, and the beauty of youth in all its gaiety and happiness, foreshadowed the beauty of heaven'.

A Greek view of the meaning of life and death with its 'uncertainties in the present' and its questioning of the future was irresistibly appealing. Pan and Hermes became divine playmates, easily crossing the boundaries of dream, and he could almost mesmerise himself into visionary moments of identification with them. At the climax to Chapter XIX dealing with his 'apostasy', Reid reaches a crisis. His passionate identification with the Greek world of the spirit leads him, he thinks, to the very brink of a mystical experience. The dreaming boy is on the point of breaking through to the world of the Greek gods. At the

very last minute, like Orpheus on the threshold of the Underworld, his nerve fails, his vision disintegrates and is gone with the moment, 'I hesitated, blundered, drew back, failed.' The experience is pagan but the terms of struggle, signs and prayers in which it is expressed are the vocabulary of Christianity.

The language of impassioned experience drops down into bathos, the sounds of the real world break through with comic Betjeman-like associations in 'the voices and laughter of a passing boating-party'. So important was this experience on the borders of dreamland that Reid quoted the extract from *Apostate* at length in his second autobiography. In a double-take on memory it had lost none of its potency.

Within the discrepancy between rapture and bathos lie self-mockery and humour. Reid's lyrical effects in his autobiographies are constantly offset against robust comedy. 'The amusing, not to say the broadly comic side of life appealed strongly to me.' His hatred of Sundays was underscored by a sly observation that on that day 'there was an increased irritability even among the most saintly'. When asked to contribute to *Ulad*, the quarterly journal of the Ulster Renaissance, by writing an article on 'The Future of Irish Opera', his subversive response was that he 'didn't believe in either the past, present, or future of Irish opera'. At Cambridge where he went at thirty 'too late and took my own world with me', his comic insights were mischievous and witty. After an evening strewn with orchids in Trinity Hall, observing the polished surfaces of Ronald Firbank whom Reid considered a decadent with a streak of talent, he felt he 'shouldn't have been surprised if Dorian Gray had dropped in'.

Of all his pen portraits, perhaps his characterisation of Skeat, Professor of Anglo-Saxon, is the most droll. Reid took some textual difficulties in 'early Scotch' poems to the great man who devoured them 'as if I had brought a bone to a dog. He seized on the difficulties, he worried them, he rent them to shreds, and looked delightfully happy. He ran to his bookshelves, climbed on to an arm-chair, and stood lightly poised with one foot on its back while he reached down a volume from a row near the ceiling.' The image of Skeat doing physical as well as mental acrobatics, is affectionate and bizarre at the same time.

The same wry humour is turned on himself when looking back on his personal record of friendship with people and dogs. 'I am inclined to believe that these canine friendships were more successful, and certainly far less disappointing ultimately, than any human relationships I have ever achieved.' Many of his comic effects derive from his anthropomorphic descriptions of his cats and dogs. Self-mockery again comes into play when he compares his own mania for collecting everything from matches to book illustrations of the 1860s with the mania of Nyx the terrier who collected ancient bones, a collection the adult Reid always respected. His humour could be larkish, down to playing a practical joke on some chickens who got up too early. Occasionally his jokes were savage, as in his relish when, in answer to his prayers, a neighbour's yapping dog was providentially cut in two by a tram.

Yapping dogs and rhapsody might seem like uncomfortably opposing poles. But Reid's range of language in these two autobiographies can shift seamlessly from the poetic to the colloquial. Reid's mother was 'dead against' his going to London to start a career, and Reynolds was 'blind as a bat'. Clusters of idiomatic speech are found particularly in *Private Road* when the life story becomes more memoir than autobiography. The heightened register for evoking the inner, secret self is more often poetic rather than purple, and nearly always avoids embarrassing the reader. Reid wrote without pretension 'simply to express the other, secret life, without thought of anything else'.

The directness of Reid's link with his childhood and boyhood, expressed in both heightened and mundane prose, is imprinted on the mind of the reader and somehow coalesces with our own childhood experiences, however superficially different they may have been. This is due partly to the fact that, like all the best autobiographers of childhood, Reid conveys the *angst* and the pains of growing up as well as the richness of the child's imaginative life. A. A. Milne identified exactly this duality at the heart of childhood in his own autobiography when he observed: 'Childhood is not the happiest time of one's life, but only to a child is pure happiness possible.'[27]

Readers of both Forrest Reid and A. A. Milne recognise the authenticity of their despatches from childhood. I think the role and function of the reader of his autobiographies was important to Reid. He reaches out to his readers, involves us, charms us, even plays jokes on us. He confides in us, shows us extracts from his writer's notebook, then disarmingly confesses, 'I have even tinkered with what you have just been reading.' The relationship with his reader is delicate, personal, playful. Perhaps in the external world we fulfil for him some part of the function of his ideal boyhood companion from the dream world.

Not only as readers are we drawn into the intensity of his childhood experience, but as adult readers we are flattered by the wide field of cultural references which effortlessly illumine the text. Greek mythology, German philosophy, international writers, opera, old masters, poetry from Theocritus to Rossetti give an almost multi-media appeal to these varied autobiographical pages. Sometimes the cultural, the real and the dream worlds spark off one another, so that the woman he is forbidden to visit in the forest has the monumental sensuousness of a Frans Hals painting, and the aged Professor Skeat is pinned in the memory for ever as 'Blake's drawing of the Ancient of Days'.

Layers of cultural comparisons are integrated in Reid's autobiographical writing – to recreate the golden dreamworld of childhood that nourished his later creative life. The reader is wooed and won – or nearly. Is there, perhaps, a gender problem for more than half the reading population? Do I as a woman feel cold-shouldered, even excluded? Reid faced this question when an American psychologist suggested he should write about adolescent ferment in girls as well as boys. With honesty Reid admitted his 'limitations of imagination, limitations of sympathy' when it came to girls. He made no pretence that he could overcome these limitations. Indeed his very strength lies in observing the restriction of his chosen parameters. Nevertheless, the hyperbolic dimensions of his portrait of Emma Holmes, the nurse who fed his earliest appetites for imaginative story-telling, and who could never be replaced in his heart's affections, may disturb female readers. Emma is conveyed in clichéd primal terms. Everything 'began and ended with Emma . . . Emma came first, and she remained first'. Robbed of individuality, Emma is elemental, 'like the air I breathed or the sun that warmed me'. With Emma's departure from the nursery, Reid deteriorates into 'that odious child'. The worship of Emma, 'beyond deities', is replaced by the disapproving creed of his mother who froze up the springs of love in her youngest child for years. Emma's 'mingled tenderness and wisdom' is symbolic rather than realistic. The character study does not completely convince: her actual impact on Reid's child self seems over-strained.

However, in spite of this one exception, in *Apostate* Reid's achievement is to reimagine so intensely each fibre of his young self that the reader senses a thrill and is re-awoken to his or her own childhood self. Reid reminds us that the real story of our own lives may be the *Private Road*, the internal and personal journey. If we allow him to, Reid may speak for the quiet lives of so many individuals. His triumph is that he specifies and universalises his own inner adventure which 'all along lay in the interpretation, and therefore, as it seems to me now, became really most adventurous precisely in those quieter hours

When the soul seeks to hear; when all is hushed
And the heart listens.'

Notes

1. Benvenuto Cellini, *The Autobiography*, 1558; translated by George Bull, London: Penguin, 1956.
2. Doris Lessing, *Love, Again*, London: Flamingo, 1996.
3. Doris Lessing, *Under My Skin, Volume One of my Autobiography, to 1949*, London: HarperCollins, 1994.
4. Eric Gill, *Autobiography*, London: Jonathan Cape, 1940.
5. Georgia O'Keeffe, *Georgia O'Keeffe*, New York: Viking Penguin, 1976.
6. Jean-Paul Sartre, *Words*, London: Hamish Hamilton, 1964.
7. Walter Pater, 'The Child in the House,' London: *Macmillan's Magazine*, August 1878.
8. Gwen Raverat, *Period Piece*, London: Faber & Faber, 1952.
9. Laurie Lee, *Cider with Rosie*, London: The Hogarth Press, 1959.
10. Janet Frame, *To the Is-land*, London: The Women's Press, 1982.
11. Christy Nolan, *Under the Eye of the Clock*, London: Weidenfeld & Nicolson, 1987.
12. Seamus Deane, *Reading in the Dark*, London: Jonathan Cape, 1996.
13. Katherine Mansfield, *Bliss and other stories*, London: Constable, 1920.
14. Vladimir Nabokov, *Speak, Memory*, London: Weidenfeld & Nicolson, 1967 (first published 1947).
15. Les Murray, Winner of the 1996 T.S.Eliot Poetry Prize, 'Performance', from *Subhuman Redneck Poems*, Manchester: Carcanet Press, 1996.
16. Rabindranath Tagore, *My Reminiscences*, London: Macmillan, 1917.
17. Eva Hoffman, *Lost in Translation*, London: Heinemann, 1989.
18. Alexander Herzen, *My Past and Thoughts*, 1885; translated from the Russian by J. D. Duff as *The Memoirs of Alexander Herzen*, New Haven: Yale University Press, 1923.
19. John Donne, *Sappho to Philaenis*, perhaps 1601; from John Carey (ed.), *John Donne*, Oxford and New York: Oxford University Press, 1990.
20. Thomas Traherne, *Centuries*, 1699, Oxford: The Clarendon Press, 1960.
21. Richard Jefferies, *The Story of my Heart*, London: Longman, Green, 1883.
22. Walter Pater, *Studies in the History of the Renaissance*, London and New York: Macmillan, 1873.
23. Charles Darwin, *Autobiography*, in *Life and Letters of Charles Darwin*, London: John Murray, 1876, suppressed passages not published until 1958.
24. Annie Besant, *An Autobiography*, London: T. Fisher Unwin, 1893.
25. Edmund Gosse, *Father and Son*, London: Heinemann, 1907.
26. Jeanette Winterson, *Oranges are not the only fruit*, London: Pandora, Routledge & Kegan Paul, 1985.
27. A. A. Milne, *It's Too Late Now*, London: Methuen, 1939.

6 Reid as a Collector

Robin de Beaumont

There is no doubt that Forrest Reid is remembered today in academic circles primarily as a novelist and critic, the two fields identified in the *Dictionary of National Biography* and in Kunitz & Haycroft's *Twentieth Century Authors* (1942). A small entry in each mentions Reid's interest in collecting book illustrations, that in *DNB* saying: '*Illustrators of the Sixties* (1928), a study of the Victorian artists in woodcut whose drawings he collected, remains an authoritative and original work in a little-explored field'. Though always of relatively specialised interest, it is nevertheless a field which has had its devotees, the periodic peaks identified by books written on the subject. The first of these was *English Illustration: 'The Sixties', 1857-70* by Gleeson White (sometime editor and co-founder of *The Studio*). This book first appeared in 1897 and was successful enough to reach a third impression by 1906. In 1919 the Victoria & Albert Museum issued a detailed catalogue edited by Martin Hardie, who had been at the museum since 1908 and was himself an artist, entitled *Modern Wood-Engravings* which included the museum's holdings of all the major 1860s artists.

Possibly as a result of this renewed interest, the most comprehensive exhibition yet staged, opened in 1923 at the National Gallery, Millbank (now the Tate), subsequently moving first to the Whitechapel Art Gallery, then to Birmingham, and finally, in 1925, to Glasgow. The exhibits were largely drawn from the collections of original drawings and watercolours belonging to Harold Hartley, who wrote the introduction to the catalogues, and of the original wood blocks belonging to J. N. Hart. Almost certainly as a result of the interest generated by this sudden explosion, Forrest Reid's book appeared in October 1928, a handsome quarto of 312 pages at an expensive 63s., published by the new firm of Faber & Gwyer and for which he is said to have made no less than six drafts.

In the Prolegomena, Chapter 1, Reid says his book is undertaken 'less as an essay in art-criticism and in bibliography than as a chronicle of a hobby' and that 'it seemed best to follow the impulse of the collector, while always remembering that the collection itself is a collection of the wood engravings of the sixties'. Only here does Reid identify himself as a collector, although the dust-wrapper also mentions that 'Mr Forrest Reid is a true amateur of the period – he has collected wood-engravings all his life.'

Some two years earlier, in April 1926, Constable had published Reid's short but moving autobiography *Apostate*, together with a limited edition of 50 signed copies. This covers childhood and adolescence, later life being charted in his *Private Road* of 1940. Strangely, despite his obvious passion as a collector, there is no mention of this activity in the later and larger book, and it almost looks as if, having published his *Illustrators* in 1928, he simply gave up collecting altogether, though this is apparently not the case.

As far as public acceptance is concerned, book auction records often seem to give a good indication of the popularity, or otherwise, of an author and his works and it is perhaps not without interest to note that, in the twenty years between 1971 and 1991, there are only three entries for Forrest Reid's non-bibliographical work, consisting of a copy of *A Garden by the Sea* (1918) in 1979, an inscribed copy of *The Spring Song* (1916) in 1981, and one of the 50 special copies of *Apostate* (1926) in 1986. By contrast, there are records of no fewer than 18 copies of *Illustrators of the Sixties* in those same twenty years.

As Forrest Reid appears to have left so little record of his collecting activities to posterity it may be worth reprinting here Chapter XVI of *Apostate*, as being virtually the only recorded source of information:

I don't think, in spite of my mother's suggestion, it can really have been the ghost of Uncle Henry who urged me, even in those days, to 'collect'. If it was, how he must have wept over my collections; and Professor Park's were not much better. He collected fossils, butterflies, and autographs; but perhaps, so far as the sport is concerned, it does not much matter what is collected.

For it *is* a sport; and though the 'bag' be no more than a heap of old cookery-books, or a cupboard-load of pamphlets printed in one's native town, yet just as much as for those who leave a trail of dead and wounded creatures behind them when they tramp the woods with a gun, the pleasure here, too, lies mainly in the chase. No book looks so well when you have catalogued it and placed it on its appointed shelf as it did in the dusty little shop where you first unearthed it; and the collector, like other lovers, need expect no permanent rapture. Possession will dull his zest; his passion will decline to affection; he may even prove unfaithful and follow vagrant loves; certainly the first thrill of discovery can never be recaptured.

Yet his hobby, whatever it be, does add a vast enjoyment

to life. And when the time comes for him to seek the auction rooms of Paradise that enjoyment is, as it were, released, like the sun's heat from burning coal, and spreading out into the air, generates excitement, conjecture, a pleasant flutter of catalogue leaves, a condition, in short, which is as far removed as possible from the depressing stagnation that usually accompanies death . . .

Needless to say, it was not of books, nor indeed of any objects possessing either an aesthetic or commercial value, that my first collections were composed. They were no better than the pickings of ash-pits; I was no better than a little rag-and-bone man. I collected matches, for instance. I doubt if most people suspect there are twenty varieties of matches in the world; but I knew there were more, far more, and I pursued them quietly, but with a marvellous concentration of purpose. Calamity, swift and spectacular, overtook this particular collection, which 'passed away in one high funeral gleam' more rapidly than Troy Town. On a Monday morning, with the intention of throwing it open to the public, I brought it to school in my trousers pocket. A dangerous place wherein to loose matches; but then, I had no other pockets, my upper garment being a blue jersey. Naturally, every now and again I felt to see if my matches were all right, and it was while I was doing so, and during a recital of the books of the Bible, that they suddenly ignited with a startling effect. Mabel Johnson, who was sitting next to me, screamed; I grew as red as a turkey-cock; but Miss Hardy understood that it had been an accident, and telling Mabel not to be silly, dismissed me to the lavatory to examine more closely into my damages.

My collection of nibs was just as stupid, and so were my collections of puzzles, of stamps, of wallpapers (perhaps the most idiotic of all), of posters (for though these latter may have looked well enough on hoardings, they were so big that when I had pasted the parts together I had to keep them wrapped round a pole. And yet (such is the sheepishness of human nature) all these crazes, except that of the posters, spread through the school like mumps or measles.

It was Professor Park who, with a boxful of rubbish from his own overflowing heap, and a discarded butterfly net, turned me to less innocent pursuits. On his drawing-room chimney-piece was a large gilt clock under a glass shade, and this clock was covered with dead butterflies. It represented, I imagine, his sole experiment in artistic expression, and though it fascinated me, I did not regard it as successful. Nevertheless, I too became a butterfly hunter, and a little later started a museum. I cleaned out a large press built into the wall of my bedroom, and here improved the shining hours by arranging and rearranging a dismal hoard of objects. I had covered the shelves with a layer of fine sea sand to the depth of about an inch, and on this I laid out my spoils. Unfortunately, though lavish with fossils and birds' eggs, Professor Park had given me no skeletons, and skeletons were essential. To obtain a couple I buried a dead rat and a largish fish, and afterwards dug them up, a stomach-turning task, because, as might have been expected, I dug them up a great deal too soon.

Moreover, even without skeletons, my bedroom (which was not unshared) had by this time acquired a distinctive atmosphere; and one day, after neglecting the museum for a week or two, I unlocked its doors to discover I had now not only dead but living specimens. It was the end; I quailed before the task that faced me; a sulky maid was summoned, and the museum was transported to the ash-pit.

It was in a much less ardent spirit that I started an aquarium, and when most of the inhabitants developed legs and wings and a marked distaste for what I believed to be their native element, I accepted this second slap of fortune with resignation. For a day or two our house was very like Eden, filled with a busy and harmonious humming, which was pierced every now and again by a scream from one or other of my sisters when some fat and friendly beetle alit for a moment on her head; but I was forbidden further experiments, nor did I particularly wish to try them. Dead things distressed me, and living things in bowls and cages distressed me even more. I had always had qualms about butterfly hunting, qualms about bird's-nesting, and, contrary to the laws of psychology, custom did not remove them. I had seen a moth which I had taken out from my 'killing bottle' apparently dead – which I had indeed mounted on a card, and labelled – coming to life an hour later, and promenading round the glass-lidded case with a pin still thrust through his thick hairy body. The sight filled me with horror, and completed my disgust for this kind of entomology.

There followed, I suppose, a lull in my activities; it was, at any rate, a year or two later, when I must have been fifteen, that they received a fresh stimulus, and one which, because it jumped with my own interests and inclinations, was to prove more satisfying.

I had been prowling on a wet afternoon backwards and forwards between the kitchen and the parlour, having nothing else to do. Everybody seemed cross and disobliging. My sisters refused to play cards with me; my mother had refused to give me butter and sugar to make toffee. I went upstairs to the drawing-room and improvised on the piano for a few minutes, till a not unexpected message reached me that I was either to play properly or to stop playing. I shut the piano and ascended still higher; in fact, to the very top landing, off which opened the servant's bedroom, my own bedroom, and the lumber-room. This last was an attic full of big trunks, broken furniture, old books, old clothes, and odds and ends of all sorts. It had a queer smell as I entered and closed the door behind me – a dry and slightly bitter smell, which was composed of the smells of cloth and leather and wood and paper and dust. I opened one of the boxes and the smell became intensified, and at the same time different, being mingled with the odour of camphor. I lifted out the tray of silks and ribbons, and the first thing I found underneath was a dress-suit which I knew must have belonged to my father. Before a cracked and foggy mirror I arrayed myself in this, but the trousers felt cold against my legs as I buttoned them round me, and when I postured in front of the ancient glass I became conscious of a strange and slightly ghostly sensation, not quite agreeable, and yet not strong enough to make me desist. In moving I had displaced a stack of magazines, some of which had slid to the floor. I now noticed that one of them lay open, showing a woodcut that caught my attention. The paper was toned to an ivory yellow; the design showed a little harbour with a woman and a child walking by the water's edge, and a man standing on the wharf, holding a bag on a truck. In the background were the black naked ropes and masts and spars of boats, and the whole thing seemed to me charming.[1]

There and then, under the sunless pallor of the skylight, I sat down and looked for other drawings. There were plenty, for there were heaps of these old magazines – *Good Words*, *Cornhills*, *Quivers*, *Argosys*, *Once a Weeks*. To me they were treasure trove. I had never been in a picture gallery in my life (because there was none in my native town); with the exceptions of Millais, and Holman Hunt, and such old *Punch* friends as du Maurier and C. K., I had never heard of the artists over whose work I now pored. Nor was my pleasure lessened when in a flash I saw here the nucleus of a new collection – a real collection this time, not a mere accumulation of rubbish. In a remarkably few minutes I had changed back into my clothes, but not before my original plan of rushing downstairs to ask my mother to give me these magazines had had time to appear over sanguine. She would ask me what I wanted them for, and when I said I wanted the pictures would tell me I could look at them as often as I liked. Even if she gave them to me she would still desire to know what I was going to do with them, and at the first mention of scissors there would be an end of my collection. She would not understand my purpose, and would regard it as mere destructiveness. She would be backed up by my sisters too, who would be sure to suggest a hospital, or the Deaf and Dumb Institution, or something of the kind. The suggestion would not be prompted by the least interest in the deaf and dumb, nor would the deaf and dumb be the least interested in Pinwell's drawings; but all the same they would get them. It would be better not even to borrow the scissors, I now saw, or rather not to mention I was borrowing them. Once I had my pictures ready, the secret would have to be revealed, for I could not mount them up here where there was no table; but I did not dwell on this, I thought only of the hours and days of enjoyment before me. So I slipped downstairs for the scissors, and without further ado settled to my task.

In the lumber-room it was cold, for these were October days, and it would have been nicer to have worked on the hearthrug in front of the dining-room fire, and under the benevolent supervision of Tabby's successor; but I dursn't risk it, so I worked on a low wooden box under the skylight, and when it became too dark to see I lit a candle. The candle shed a forlorn light across the mingle-mangle of variegated litter, creating shadows which were out of all proportion black and solid. Not a sound reached me, not a sound in the candle-lit stillness but the rustle of paper and the snip-snip of my scissors. There had been a time when I should not have sat there so tranquilly, I thought; for lumber-rooms were well known to be dubious places, attractive to the ghostly owners of the shrouded spoils they held as, decked in my father's clothes I had mimed and preened myself in front of that cracked mirror, subconsciously, and not so very subconsciously perhaps, it had really been the notion that his face might peep over my shoulder which had made me uneasy. But there was nothing in such moon-and-green-cheese stuff, I now told myself, and, though the fact that it should have occurred to me at all rather contradicted this bold intellectual scepticism, I worked on in my den – a thought uneasily it may be – till the ringing of a bell called me down to light and warmth and the cheerful noise of a large family gathered round a tea-table . . .

Meanwhile, in the black-and-white art of the sixties I became from day to day more versed. Pinwell (my first discovery), Boyd Houghton, Fred Walker, J. D. Watson, Sandys, North, Arthur Hughes – these and others were soon as familiar to me as my own. And C. K., who had always been my favourite, whose jokes were better than anybody else's, turned out to be Charles Keene, who could make beautiful drawings as well as comic ones. The majority of the designs were illustrations for serial stories. There were William Small's drawings for *Griffith Gaunt*; du Maurier's for *Eleanor's Victory*, *Foul Play*, and *Wives and Daughters*; Charles Keene's for *A Good Fight* and *Evan Harrington*; Millais's and Fred Walker's for the tales of Miss Martineau and the novels of Trollope; Pinwell's and Arthur Hughes's for stories by George Macdonald. These woodcuts possessed an increasing fascination for me. They accepted life as it was and turned it into beauty; they invested the most homely material with a delicate and poetic charm.

So I cut out and mounted my pictures, carefully dating each drawing, and writing its title at the foot of the board, and the title of the magazine in which I had found it. My collection began to grow bulk, though it was limited to the spoils of the lumber-room. As for those volumes which I saw priced at a few pence on second-hand-book stalls – I had no money to buy one of them.

This, then, appears to be the only first-hand account we have of Forrest Reid's collecting, and such information as to how his collection grew, details of any exciting chases, alterations in direction, or bitter disappointments – the pattern and interest of all collectors' lives – remain shrouded in mystery. There appear to be no public records of his purchases or disposals, or any of the information which adds to our knowledge of this facet of his life, which, by the evidence of the remains, must have consumed a considerable amount of his time. What is known is that he presented his collection of the cut out and neatly mounted illustrations from the Sixties magazines to the Ashmolean in 1946, the year before his death, and that his friend and fellow Ulsterman, John Bryson, the author of his entry in *DNB* and a Fellow of Balliol College, Oxford, himself a collector of Pre-Raphaelite pictures and drawings which are now also in the Ashmolean, was the link which brought this about.

Some eighteen years after Forrest Reid's death, Sotheby's held a book sale at their New Bond Street premises from 1 to 3 March 1965. One of the six named properties, which included books from the library of Sir Osbert Sitwell, was from the Executors of the late J. N. Hart, the lender of the wood blocks to the 1923 National Gallery exhibition, and consisted of lots 83-100 for sale on the first day. The larger part of Hart's library had previously appeared on 3 February, and consisted of 198 lots, mostly single early books, or Doves Press, and with only a few minor Sixties books in no more than half-a-dozen lots out of the total. In this second sale, however, lots 83-93 were all early books, with three incunables and a folio printing by Wynken de Worde of John Capgrave's *Nova Legende Anglie* 1516 (£85 to Marlborough), only beaten in price by a 1637 Camden *Britain* translated by Philemon Holland which went to an R. Nicholson for £160. The remainder, lots 94 to 110, obviously considered the dross and lumped together at the end, were entered as:

A Collection of Victorian Illustrated Books. The following seventeen lots, contain a large number of books collected by Forrest Reid in connection with his *Illustrations of the Sixties*, many of them with his signature. The collection was extended by the late Mr.Hart.

Of these, lot 94 consisted of three folios – a presentation copy to E. J. Pointer (sic) of Dalziel's *Bible Gallery* (1880), [recte (1881)]; and the companion reprints, both limited editions, of Birket Foster's *Pictures of English Landscape* (1881), and *English Rustic Pictures* (1882). Lots 95 (20 vols) & 96 (37 vols) were Dalziel Brothers' books and included five presentation copies from the Dalziels themselves, together with four of their own copies which had five ALS's (autograph letters, signed) inserted. Lot 97 was a copy of the Doyle/Leigh *Manners and Customs of the English* (1849); and other lots included a 42-vols collection of works by T. A. Guthrie ('F. Anstey'); 20 vols illustrated or written by Laurence Housman; two lots comprising Samuel Palmer's *Eclogues of Virgil* (1883) and

Shorter Poems of Milton (1889); a collection of Phil May books, with albums of cartoons and typed indexes, all belonging to Forrest Reid; two lots of 19 vols of Ruskin and associated works; and four lots totalling 17 vols which included the Gleeson White and Forrest Reid books on the subject, and complementary bibliography on Keene, Shields, Houghton etc. However, by far the largest lot was 102, described as follows:

Nineteenth Century Book Illustration. A collection of over four hundred volumes and bound periodicals with illustrations by J. E. Millais, Walter Crane, Birket Foster, George du Maurier, John Tenniel, Arthur Hughes, A. B. Houghton and others, *the majority Forrest Reid's copies, with his signatures, sold as a collection, not subject to return. various sizes (a stack).*
(their italics)

At the time I was working for a firm of architects in Mason's Yard, off Duke Street, St James's, a brisk five-minute walk from Sotheby's. Every lunch 'hour' (for no doubt this must have been somewhat extended, work presumably being in one of the slump periods, so frequently alternating with boom, of the time) I spent examining the collection. I still retain the pencil notes that I made of the 'stack', as well as others from the Sixties' lots, notes which I rewrote at the time in alphabetical order by title in ink, recording briefly variant bindings with binders' tickets and, in particular, those with Forrest Reid's signature and condition. Sorting these out over thirty years later I find I have records of only 365, from the 'over four hundred' of these Sixties books, of which 143 had his signature, none with his bookplate, and the condition frequently being recorded as 'poor' or 'shabby'. Very occasionally there is a note of 'very fine' or 'brilliant' and, curiously, any of the high-spots like Millais's *Parables of Our Lord*, or *Wayside Posies*, or *Home Thoughts and Home Scenes*, turn out not to be the ones with Reid's signature. Those with Dalziel bookplates, with letters from artists, or presentation copies from publishers or wood-engravers, are even less likely to be amongst those with Forrest Reid's signature, so one starts to wonder just how true it is that the collection was basically his. Surely, if the high-spots had been his, he would have recorded his ownership with his signature on these rather than, as occurs, on some nonentity like Mrs Cupple's *The Story of Our Doll* (Nelson, 1873), or on the standard Dickens' *Household Editions*, all of which bear his distinctive diagonal signature, or on the shabby, undated, undistinguished reissue of Pennell's *Pegasus Re-Saddled*, rather than on the finer, unsigned copy of the first?

I must have been allowed access to make my records prior to the sale for at least a fortnight, long enough for me to also make a note of those copies which I would like to have bought. These seem to have been three from lot 95, nine from lot 96 and no less than thirty-eight from lot 102, as well as three from the Housman collection. In the event lots 94 (£24) and 95 (£60) as well as 101 (£30), together with the stack, lot 102 (£170), were bought by

Pickering & Chatto acting for an American collector and philanthropist, Gordon M. Ray, who gave them to the Pierpont Morgan Library of New York. A subsequent attempt to acquire at least a few of the duplicates directly from him met with a friendly but negative response in a letter of 19 July 1966. 'I regret to say that it is beyond my power to assist you in the way you request. I collected '60's books for some years before my sweep at Sotheby's. Finding myself with nearly 100 duplicates after this purchase, I sent the lot to Princeton University, where there is a large collection of such books, hence I have nothing to offer you. The best I can do, I am afraid, is to send you a xerox copy of North's letter of 1 December 1867 laid in *The Spirit of Praise*. With all good wishes . . .' Lot 96, however, went to Max Brimmell and here I was fortunate enough to acquire all nine items I wanted from him, as well as the three from the Housman lot which had been bought by Francis Edwards.

So was dispersed, ignominiously and with absolutely no interest from 'The Establishment', the last of the great Sixties' collections, following on the tradition of neglect accorded to its predecessors. These had included the remains of the Dalziel archive, the bulk of which were already housed in the Department of Prints and Drawings at the British Museum, which had been dispersed, piecemeal, by an eccentric Charing Cross Road dealer in the 1950s after having been offered to, and largely declined by, the Victoria & Albert Museum. The Harold Hartley collection, arguably the finest ever of original drawings and sketches, which had provided the bulk of the 1923 National Gallery, Millbank (Tate) Exhibition, as well as thirty-four (as against Hart's seventeen) illustrations to Forrest Reid's book, had been bought by a perceptive Curator of Art at the Boston Museum of Fine Arts, Henry P. Rossiter, in 1955 for the asking price of £3 000 (about £32 000 today), again after having been first offered, unsuccessfully, to British institutions. They were, of course, deeply unfashionable at the time in the brave post-war new world of glass and concrete. However, by 1965 one might, perhaps, just have hoped for more understanding of the High Victorian. It certainly had its appreciators in America.

It still seemed unclear as to what had actually happened to Forrest Reid's collection after his death in 1947. Obviously Hart, a much younger friend, had acquired the collection after Reid's death, but it seems, according to Brian Taylor who has kindly allowed me to use the information he has gathered, that the collection was in fact left first to an older friend and must somehow have been acquired by Hart subsequently. Hart had his own book-plate designed by Stephen Gooden and obviously cared for condition whereas, on the evidence of the piles of books in Sotheby's, Forrest Reid seems never to have used a bookplate and appeared to have had scant regard for condition, apparently collecting books mainly for academic purposes. It therefore came as something of a surprise to learn from Brian Taylor that this was far from the case, that Reid did indeed care much for condition, wrapping each book in a plain paper dust-wrapper to preserve it, and that almost certainly something happened during the period between his death and Hart's acquisition which accounted for the sad deterioration of his collection. Though the full story cannot yet be told, it does seem possible that for a time the books were left under a tarpaulin in a farmyard barn.

As the story unfolded, it seemed to me that it would be of interest to try and find out a little more about Mr Hart. On one of the pages of my Sotheby's 1965 notes I had written 'Harman Hart Esq. Lochinver, Little Heath, Heath Road, Potters Bar, Middx.' Just why I did not remember, but it seemed as good a lead as any and so, thirty-one years later, I rang directory enquiries for the number of the local public library. Lochinver turned out to be a school and a member of staff suggested I contact Mr Brian Warren of the Potters Bar & District Historical Society who turned out to be most helpful. He unearthed an entry in the *Barnet Press* of August 1921 about the death of Mr John Samuel Hart of Lochinver and another for January 1975 about the death of Miss Mary Anne (Queenie) Hart, John Samuel's daughter, who had come with her parents and brothers, Jack and Lionel, from Reigate to Barnet some time before the First World War and lived at Lochinver, now Lochinver House School. According to Queenie's obituary notice of 31 January 1975 in the *Barnet Press*, she and her brother Jack (our John N. Hart) had 'built Meadow House in the mid-1930's beside what was to become their attractive rose garden, choosing suitable bricks and other materials for their Queen Anne-style house. There they had collections of pictures, snuff boxes, china and jade which have been given to the Victoria and Albert Museum.' With this clue, I got on to the V & A where, with the help of Anna Jackson and Andrew Bolton of the Far Eastern Department, I found the original correspondence between the solicitors acting for J. N. Hart's estate. In a letter of 19 November 1963 the senior partner, Mr F. B. Cockburn informs the Museum that they have been left a gold and silver St George cigarette case made for Hart by Omar Ramsden, and that he instructed

the Executors to offer to the Trustees his Proof Set of Dalziel's *Bible Gallery* which formerly belonged to Sir E. J. Poynter, R. A., [and] his Collection of Wood Blocks for the Dalziel *Bible Gallery* and Millais *Parables*. Unlike the bequest of the Omar Ramsden Cigarette Case, which has no strings attached, the offer of the Dalziel *Bible Gallery*, etc., is expressed to be conditional upon your Trustees giving to the Executors an undertaking in writing that at least one-tenth of the Collection shall be always on view to the public, and that the Collection shall be known and described as the 'J. N. Hart Bequest'. In the event of your Trustees declining this bequest, the Executors are to offer it to the Trustees of the Tate Gallery upon similar terms, and if they should decline, to the Trustees of the British Museum without any conditions attached.

Sotheby's valued the cigarette case at £30, and the *Bible Gallery* with two sets of original wood blocks at £25. The gift of the gold and silver cigarette case was accepted, but Sir Trenchard Cox, the Director of the Museum, was unwilling to comply with the conditions attached on the rest and the offer was therefore declined. Nevertheless Mr Cockburn refused to give up and in a further letter of 30 January 1964 to Cox he writes:

I am concerned for the Executors of the late Mr J. N. Hart, who during the course of his life made a number of Collections of one kind or another, and by his Will directed his Trustees to offer various items to specified Museums, and the rest of his Collections he left to his Executors to sell to their best advantage, giving them power to decide what, when and where to sell, and further authorising them to sell at less than market price or in certain circumstances to give items to Museums if the result could be said to enhance the value of such a Collection. The Executors are further permitted to lend items to Museums for such time as they may think fit, or even to lend the whole of the Testator's Collection for exhibition purposes.

He then goes on to list eight areas 'the Testator seems to have collected' which included original letters of Charles Lamb, engravings of Stephen Gooden, Martinware, and a miscellaneous collection of watercolours, principally those of G. J. Pinwell and Stanley Anderson. In a hand-written last page Cockburn says to Cox, 'Indeed I'm writing to you in the first place largely as a result of your obituary note in The Times. He was a nice person, and happy as he was in his chosen occupations, we couldn't but feel from time to time that he was a lonely man – increasingly so as the years passed. This was probably why he always seemed to me to value friendship so highly that he was almost reluctant to give as much of himself as he could for fear that he might over-cultivate his friends.'

By April 1964 the Museum wrote that they were willing to buy a chalice and cover by Oman for £40 and added that 'If, by any chance, there were also a possibility that the Executors might offer us some of the items as gifts, the following would be very gratefully received in our collections: (1) two G. J. Pinwell watercolours 'The Bailiff' and 'A Lake with figures' . . . and (2) two items of the Martinware . . . being a small fish-figure and a vase, decorated with representations of crabs.' Consequently the *Bible Gallery* was rejected by the V & A, which, apart from the conditions attached, already had a copy, and so this presentation copy inscribed to Poynter was the one which duly appeared as lot 94, in the Sotheby's sale of Monday, 1 March 1965. From the description, 'unbound in original portfolio, vellum spine and flap', this must have been one of the very limited copies, even larger and more limited than the vellum-bound 'Large Paper' copies.

One possible lead in this attempt to find out more about Mr Hart and the source of his collection seemed to me to be the *Times* obituary notice, by no less a figure than the Director and Secretary of the V & A, mentioned in the solicitor's letter of 30 January 1964. I began my search by obtaining a copy of John Napthali Hart's death certificate from which I learnt that he died on 10 June 1963 at the age of 81. A subsequent exhaustive search through *The Times* from then up to the date of the solicitor's letter yielded absolutely no clue as to its location, and, although there certainly was an obituary by Trenchard Cox within those dates, it had absolutely nothing to do with Hart. Perhaps, tucked away in some paragraph there is a mention, but I have been unable to find it, and, for the moment at any rate, the full story of what happened to Forrest Reid's collection from his death to its appearance in Sotheby's so many years later remains a mystery.

Again, just how many of the books included in the Sotheby's sale comprised those 'extended by the late Mr. Hart', at this distance we shall probably never know. Nevertheless it seems safe to say that this combined collection constituted one of the finest and most comprehensive ever formed of the books of the wood-engraved illustrators of the period, the like of which we are unlikely ever to see again and that Forrest Reid will be remembered not only for his work as a novelist, but also for this collection and for the book which resulted from it. The eleven-page Appendix alone in *Illustrators of the Sixties*, with its listing of over four hundred of the books of the period, has provided the impetus for at least one devotee to hunt for them continuously over the past thirty years – and he still continues to do so.

Note

1. This is Pinwell's illustration for George Macdonald's 'Guild Court' in *Good Words* for November 1867, p.781.

7 Reid and Illustration

Paul Goldman

They approached the long, low house by a path that led through a sweetly-smelling, trim and brilliant garden. A gardener was mowing the grass at the side of the house, and the hum of the machine rose sleepily through the heat of the cloudless afternoon. There was for Rusk an old-fashioned charm about the place – about the house with its drapery of creepers, about the garden, even about the mellow sunlight on the grass and on the flower-beds – which seemed to make it an ideal spot wherein two elderly maiden ladies might pass their quiet lives. It all reminded him – with an odd jump back to other days – of the illustrations to certain mid-Victorian poems and tales which in his childhood, on wet afternoons, he had now and then been allowed to colour - pictures found in old magazines, wood-engravings by Millais or Pinwell or Fred Walker.

The imaginative illustration of literature, as this quotation from one of his novels eloquently reveals, was for Reid a subject which went beyond fascination – it suffused his very being. Although the extract is taken from a rewritten novel not published until 1947,[1] the original work appeared in 1911, some seventeen years before the appearance of *Illustrators of the Sixties*. In this latter volume there is an echo of the former where Reid takes the amateur colourist very firmly to task.

In his chapter entitled 'On Collecting, Collections, and Selections' he thunders: 'A further destructive agent is the nursery artist. This little pest was ever ready with his brushes and his box of water-colours. When he has adorned only a single design in a rare book it is tempting to try to remove his handiwork, but personally I have found such efforts unavailing, and it is better to make up one's mind never to buy an imperfect book no matter how many years one may have been searching vainly for a sound copy.'[2] The link between the two publications is both amusing and instructive. In the novel Reid is appealing to the imagination. In the work of criticism he is sounding a warning – a comment intended both to alert the collector and also to plead for conservation. However, he is not entirely consistent, as the Ashmolean collection bears witness, for it is essentially a highly organised accumulation of magazine illustrations cut from their pages by Reid for study and reference and now housed in some fifty boxes. Nevertheless, he wrote of this material:

The magazines present a difficult problem. They are essential to a collection that pretends to any degree of completeness, but on the other hand they take up a great deal of room, and it is extremely tedious to have to turn over several hundred pages for the sake of perhaps a dozen, perhaps only two or three, drawings. To those whose shelf room is limited the temptation to extract the prints worth extracting becomes almost irresistible, and as far as the collector himself is concerned this course is undoubtedly the more satisfactory. Not only will he be able to classify his drawings, but the drawings themselves will look much better when mounted separately on white boards than when wedged between unattractive slabs of letterpress. The margin of the board supplies at once a foil to the tint of the paper and a frame, showing the whole picture to the best advantage. Yet, to mutilate a volume of *The Cornhill* or *Good Words* is an act of vandalism, to say nothing of the really rare magazines. In the case of a magazine like *Good Words for the Young* it is hoped that nobody will think of doing so, any more than of cutting up a volume of *Punch*. After all, the original setting has an interest of its own, and as time passes this interest increases.[3]

Thus, somewhat contrarily, Reid did not take his own advice except in one significant respect. He evidently refrained from dismembering any copies of *Good Words for the Young* which may explain why Arthur Hughes's memorable designs for George Macdonald's *At the Back of the North Wind* are not to be found in the Oxford collection. Reid was, after all, only imitating, to an extent, suggestions made by Gleeson White many years before.[4] The results of such activities have proved little short of disastrous, for bound runs of these periodicals are now extremely rare, and this makes reuniting image and text a lengthy and often complex process. That the advice has been taken to heart by other collectors can be seen by the presence of similar collections of periodical designs almost identically organised and mounted elsewhere.[5]

Whatever current thinking may be about the preservation of illustrated magazines, the collection in Oxford provides an opportunity to make these images known to a wider public. It also permits a revealing glimpse into the mind of a highly creative writer and commentator. For Reid was essentially a consummate discriminator and his eye for quality is apparent both in the collection itself and even more clearly in the book, which forms the basis of the present catalogue. Here he judiciously arranged the artists into groups, and the definition of 'The Idyllic School' is an invention which we can largely attribute to Reid himself. In addition, however, he dignified the entire subject of the illustrators of the Sixties and his work has remained essential for all later scholars and critics. Much of his philosophy on the subject may be found in his early chapters, and indeed his thoughts can almost be entirely crystallised by a quotation. Reid bravely and, even in 1928, somewhat controversially defends sentiment when speaking of these wood-engravings, having already noted that the artists' 'methods have fallen into temporary disrepute'.

Take Ghirlandajo's [sic] famous portrait of the bottle-nosed old man and his grandson: – does not much of its charm lie in the relation of trust and affection that obviously exists between the old man and the child; lie, that is to say, in its sentiment? It is certainly there, the dreaded quality, yet, being the expression of an emotion that is true and fine, it becomes a part of the picture's beauty; in other words, possesses a definitely aesthetic value.[6]

Reid continues to argue, against Whistler, on behalf of respecting and honouring the subject in art. In short, he is demanding that illustration be taken seriously as a branch of art rather than dismissed as decoration or excrescence, 'for if a picture be not devoid of any intellectual, spiritual, and emotional content, its subject *must* contribute to the appeal it makes'. He continues, quoting Rembrandt's later portraits, which he sees as 'portraits of the soul as much as of the body . . . This penetration, this gift of imaginative sympathy, is an essential part of the artist's equipment, of his genius, and without it that genius would be so much the poorer.'[7] Thus we can see something of what Reid was thinking about when he decided to write his book, but it still remains to examine why so unassuming a study should have become both a classic of its kind and a standard work of reference.

The 1860s in England saw a remarkable increase in black and white illustration to works of literature contained in both books and periodicals. The reasons for this phenomenon are both many and complex. Changes in economics, education, communication and the technology of printing all had parts to play, and this brief essay is not the place to rehearse them in detail.[8] However, what clearly appealed to Reid's highly developed artistic sensibilities was the fact that so many distinguished artists produced such a wealth of magnificent designs. The movement (if indeed it may be termed one) was led by the Pre-Raphaelite artists, notably Rossetti, Millais and Holman Hunt. Within a few years another group which Reid classified as the 'Idyllic School' followed, and this encompassed practitioners such as Arthur Boyd Houghton, George Pinwell and Frederick Walker. In addition numerous other artists, several of the highest distinction, turned, at least for a time, to providing imaginative illustrations to literature. Among these were Whistler, Poynter, and perhaps Reid's favourite, the ubiquitous Charles Keene.

The distinguished predecessor to Reid's work was written by Gleeson White in 1897 (see note 4). This was essentially an encyclopaedia of designs, and, even after a century, it remains useful for its inclusive character and a judicious choice of photographs. However, White, at least in this volume, was a compiler before he was an analyst. In complete contrast, Reid produced a study which was

quintessentially critical and literary. He was unduly modest when he proclaimed that his book was 'undertaken less as an essay in art-criticism and in bibliography than as the chronicle of a hobby.'[9] Instead Reid created a work that became the source book for generations of collectors and enthusiasts up to the present time. Indeed Robin de Beaumont, who presented his collection to the British Museum Department of Prints and Drawings in 1992, formed his exemplary group of books largely on the basis of Reid's checklist which appeared as the conclusion to his text. Reid was particularly well qualified to write such a book. Not only was he steeped in the knowledge of the designs themselves, as recalled in *Apostate* (see Chapter 6) but he was also exceptionally widely read in the literature of the mid-nineteenth century which they accompanied.

Unlike most contemporary art-historians, Reid possessed an intimate familiarity with the stories of writers such as George Macdonald, Dinah Mulock (Mrs Craik) and Miss Braddon. Surely only Reid could have remarked of du Maurier's designs for Florence Montgomery's *Misunderstood* (1874),

The *Misunderstood* drawings, have, I think, been over-praised. They are graceful, and several of them are brilliantly pretty, but the faults in the tale happen to be those which to du Maurier would appear as virtues and he has accented them. The small hero is supposed to be a scapegrace – a scapegrace who is constantly getting into scrapes of the kind that amuse grown-up readers. When du Maurier presents him in picture after picture always in immaculate velveteens and with never a curl out of place the last rag of verisimilitude is sacrificed.[10]

There is yet another important reason why the book has stood the test of time. In addition to the cogency of argument and the profound acquaintance with both the literature and the art, Reid's work is outstandingly accurate. Unlike White, he is fastidious over dates of publication and other minutiae essential to bibliographers. His insistence on first editions is not pedantry and he makes a powerful case for it.

But the desire for 'firsts', I think, can here for once be defended on rational grounds, since nearly invariably (there are exceptions which I shall note) the earliest printings from the blocks are the best, and certainly some of the late printings are markedly inferior. Now and again, indeed, in a very late issue they are hardly recognisable. I have before me *A Picture Book* published by Routledge in 1879, in which the designs, for the most part by William Small, have, through too frequent service, lost every quality they once possessed.[11]

Reid's major achievement was to recognise and to document an area of English art which too frequently has been judged to be minor or esoteric. His comments remain valuable because he is just to all and never over-praises. He does not write in jargon and on occasion his perception is both telling and unforgettable. One notable such moment occurs in the section on George Pinwell, a much loved artist though frequently faulty. Reid remarked, 'The work of an artist like Pinwell is always liable to be over- or underestimated. It is an art extremely personal in its manner and therefore in its appeal; it is an art hampered constantly by an imperfect technique, and yet its very failures are frequently more interesting than the successes of cleverer draughtsmen, while its successes are lovely as April primroses.'[12] Although this is a far cry from current critical fare, it is a reasoned judgement which by reason of its poetry lodges in the memory.

Reid's checklist of illustrated books, although somewhat idiosyncratically arranged by title rather than by author, works well and is almost invariably correct, while the main index is impeccable. Reid provides in this work a quarry of material and information which has proved useful and inspirational to all successive commentators. Without its magisterial presence there is little doubt that the talents of many of the illustrators here chronicled would have remained for ever entombed and unappreciated in obscure volumes and forgotten periodicals.

Bibliography

Forrest Reid, writings on illustration:

Illustrators of the Sixties, London: Faber & Gwyer, 1928.
'Charles Keene, Illustrator', in *Print Collector's Quarterly*, January 1930, pp. 23-47.
'The line engravings of Stephen Gooden', in *Print Collector's Quarterly*, January 1932, pp.51-73.

Further reading on illustration of the sixties:

Percy Muir, *Victorian Illustrated Books*, London: Batsford, 1971.
Simon Houfe, *The Dictionary of British Book Illustrators and Caricaturists 1800-1914*, Woodbridge, Suffolk: Antique Collectors' Club, 1978, revised 1981, 1996.
Eric de Maré, *The Victorian Woodblock Illustrators*, London: Gordon Fraser, 1980.
Paul Goldman, *Victorian Illustration – The Pre-Raphaelites, the Idyllic School and the High Victorians*, Aldershot: Scolar Press, 1996.
All the above contain extensive bibliographies.

Notes

1. *Denis Bracknel - A Family Chronicle*, London: Faber & Faber, 1947, p.65. The book was re-written by Reid from *The Bracknels: A Family Chronicle*, London: Edward Arnold, 1911.
2. *Illustrators of the Sixties*, London: Faber & Gwyer, 1928, p.7.
3. *Illustrators*, p.11.
4. Gleeson White, *English Illustration 'The Sixties': 1855-70*, London: Archibald Constable and Co., 1897; reprinted 1906, p.7.
5. Examples are to be found in the Department of Prints and Drawings at the British Museum, the Hunterian Art Gallery, Glasgow and the Print Collection of the University College of Wales, Aberystwyth.
6. *Illustrators*, p.2.
7. *Illustrators*, p.4.
8. For a lengthy discussion of these matters, see Paul Goldman, *Victorian Illustrated Books 1850 – 1870 – The Heyday of Wood-Engraving*, London: British Museum Press, 1994.
9. *Illustrators*, p.1.
10. *Illustrators*, p.185.
11. *Illustrators*, pp.7-8.
12. *Illustrators*, p.152.

8 Forrest Reid and Walter de la Mare: a Literary Friendship

Anne Harvey

I can remember a winter afternoon many years ago, in the University Library at Cambridge, when I was prowling round the shelves upstairs and took down by the merest chance a thin pale-blue volume called *Songs of Childhood*, by Walter Ramal. I had never heard of Walter Ramal, and the book opened at this poem:

> Sailorman, I'll give to you
> My bright silver penny,
> If out to sea you'll sail me
> And my dear sister, Jenny

I don't know if my reader will have had a similar experience, and I cannot now from the *Songs of Childhood* itself quite recapture it, but it was as if in the silence and fading light of that deserted library, I had, like some adventurer in the Middle Ages, sailed all unexpectedly into sight of an unknown and lovely shore. Apart from everything else there was this thrill of a complete newness. I read on and on. I hunted in the catalogue for other books by Walter Ramal. He had written one other, *Henry Brocken*. In the meantime, on my way back to my rooms, I ordered this book and got it two days later. Thus it was that for many years *Songs of Childhood* held a kind of jealous place in my affections – even up till the publications of *The Listeners* and *Peacock Pie* – for an impression so vivid is hard to dislodge.

That was how Forrest Reid described his first encounter with Walter de la Mare, then writing under his pseudonym, in his critical study of the poet, published in 1929.[1] Sixteen years earlier, in the spring of 1913, the friendship between the two writers began, a friendship described by Theresa Whistler, de la Mare's biographer, as 'his closest work friendship of his next thirty years'.[2]

In 1912 de la Mare had received an undated letter of admiration from Forrest Reid, along with a copy of Reid's novel *The Bracknels*. The envelope was later marked: 'FR's first letter to me – keep.'

Dear Sir, . . . I hope you will accept this little tale which I venture to send you in token of my admiration of your beautiful books. Believe me, yours very truly,
Forrest Reid.

De la Mare, unsure as to the sex of the writer, merely acknowledged this, and on 1 June 1912 Reid wrote again from 9 South Parade, Belfast:

I should like to express my gratitude for your new book of poems [*The Listeners*] . . . Many of them I think, have an exquisite beauty and originality and all have, for me at least, that mysterious quality of charm . . .

Mentioning that he had reviewed the book, he added: 'I

do not suppose that you take much interest in such things, but if you should gather from them that I wish you well . . . that is all I desire'.

De la Mare was pleased with this and now hoped that the two might meet. He told Reid: 'At present I am drudging as reader to Heinemann and if you are not bound to any publisher and have a manuscript awaiting publication, I wonder if you would like to send it to me.'

He was too late. Reid's novel, *Following Darkness* was already with Arnold, and de la Mare later reviewed it. He wrote personally to Reid: 'What I have read has been a kind of personal pleasure and recognition, difficult to put into words.'

Theresa Whistler explains this as 'a strong, curious shock of affinity he felt, more intimate, in this unknown Ulsterman's work, than he had ever felt before'. This was, of course, exactly how Reid had felt in the Cambridge Library and when they met at last they were not disappointed in each other.

Their meeting-place was that popular haunt of the literary circles of the time, St George's Cafe in St Martin's Lane. Here, too, W. H. Davies, Ralph Hodgson, Edward Thomas and John Freeman met, and here the American poet, Robert Frost, was welcomed on his visit to England. It was a good place to discover the personalities, characters and foibles of fellow writers in a relaxed, congenial atmosphere.

Russell Burlingham describes Forrest Reid as

of middle height and rather stockily built, his movements emphatic rather than graceful. But it was his face which attracted your attention: not handsome indeed, even perhaps rather ugly, but ugly in a friendly, blunt-featured, attractive fashion. Square high forehead, kindly, ironical eyes, the nose rather broad, and the Ulsterman's long sardonic upper lip – these were the characteristics which first struck those who met him. In middle life it was his habit to wear pince-nez and, before he started using the normal horn-rimmed glasses, this gave him an aspect careful and almost professorial, belying the great natural force of his features. His clothes were a little old-fashioned, and for the most part he wore the familiar, narrow, rather short blue suit with baggy pockets and something of the air of outworn schooldays about it.

Walter de la Mare was of similar height, stockily built but nimble. Naomi Royde-Smith, literary editor of the *Saturday Westminster*, described him as 'a round little man in a round little coat' but further inspection made her think of the face of a Roman emperor, 'dark, slightly curling hair, brown, almost golden eyes, and an enchanting smile. His faun's ears stood out a little from the side of his head. His blue serge suit with a round jacket gave him a faintly nautical air and he was far from silent.'

I wonder if de la Mare would have gone out of his way to discover the lesser-known Belfast writer for himself, or if Reid's initiative was needed to prompt the friendship. There were, undoubtedly, similar interests to draw them together. In 1913 de la Mare was forty, Reid two years younger. The Celtic Twilight cult in literature with its emphasis on Beauty, the Natural World and Pan attracted even the level-headed and sceptical. Pan had always held a secure place in poetry; Marvell's 'The garden', Shelley's 'Hymn to Pan', and Keats's 'Endymion' all featured him, and in 1844 Elizabeth Barrett Browning based 'The Dead Pan' on Plutarch's legend bemoaning the exodus of Dryads and Oreads and the Silence of the Gods of Hellas:

> Do ye leave your rivers flowing
> All alone, O Naiad,
> While your drenched locks dry slow in
> This cold feeble sun and breeze?
> Not a word the Naiads say,
> Though the rivers run for aye,
>   For Pan is dead ....

And she followed this, in 1862, with

> What was he doing, the Great God Pan,
> Down in the reeds by the river?

The master of this genre of the macabre and the supernatural, Arthur Machen, had published *The Great God Pan* in 1894, and, ten years earlier, J. M. Barrie's *Peter Pan* was first produced on the London stage. The 'boy who never grew up' was named after Pan, symbol of Nature, Paganism and the Amoral World, and in the same year *The Independent Review* published E. M. Forster's 'The Story of a Panic'.

These influences were especially relevant to Reid's 1905 novel, *The Garden God*, where the main character, Graham, recalls his boyhood love for Harold Brocklehurst. In an idyllic seaside setting Graham comments that 'this place and this weather are pleasant enough for Pan'. After their bathe they sat on the rocks, baking in the hot sun.

'How brown your hands and face are!' said Graham lazily. 'The rest of you seems so white . . . I wonder if the Greeks ever made a statue of a diver? I don't remember one.' Then a sudden thought seemed to strike him and he sprang to his feet, his drowsiness suddenly gone. 'Wait a moment . . . Stand there . . . Turn round just a little . . . You must lean against the rock and hold this bit of seaweed in your hand; and you must cross your feet – like that. Oh! if you just had pointed ears or the least bit of a tail! . . . A Faun! A Faun! A young woodland Faun! . . . You are far nicer than the statue.' And a look almost of wonder came into Graham's face.

De la Mare's handling of the Pan theme seems mildly romantic beside that. In 1906 the poem 'Tears' opens with

> They told me Pan was dead, but I
>   Oft marvelled who it was that sang
> Down the green valleys languidly
>   Where the grey-elder thickets hang . . .

and next to it 'Sorcery':

> 'What voice is that I hear
>   Crying across the pool?'
> 'It is the voice of Pan you hear,
> Crying his sorceries shrill and clear,
>   In the twilight dim and cool.' [3]

Despite his 'faun's ears' de la Mare avoided, instinctively, the more sickly, cloying aspects of the god, and the poem that immediately follows these two attempts is a mysterious, cold and haunting one, 'The Children of Stare', a poem which offers the sort of background atmosphere that would later be so admired in his short stories.

It was these short stories that were always to enthral Reid, and he frequently tried to persuade de la Mare to publish a collection. Already, in July 1913, he was writing: 'What about the short stories? I think you really ought to publish them . . .'

Over the years he collected them and told his friend in November 1920:

I have The Riddle. It is cut out and put in a book – a sort of house for your neglected children. They stare out at me with forlorn and questioning faces, rather reproachfully but what can I do for them more than give them a shelter? Do you want it – this tiniest and loveliest of the company? If so, I will detach him and send him on – but not to be cast aside and lost.

De la Mare obviously accepted this offer of the neatly arranged copy of 'The Riddle', for Reid then wrote:

I send you The Riddle (which I have never solved and which you refuse to solve for me) . . . I wish, however, that you had kept The Riddle for a book of your own stories . . . its first appearance, I mean. You must have been gazing in a crystal for I have actually finished the first draft of a 'supernatural and house' tale and am trying to lock it into shape, my difficulty being that I'm not sure that I haven't been trying to tell two stories at once, with two distinct atmospheres.'

'The Riddle' had actually been written as long ago as 1898 and was included in an issue of *The Horn Book*, the household magazine made for de la Mare's young nieces and nephews. When the story was eventually published in 1923, in a collection that established his skill in this field,[4] not a word needed altering – significant for a writer who was accustomed to much revising and reworking. 'The Riddle' is short and exquisitely succinct from an opening sentence that assumes the reader's prior knowledge: 'So these seven children, Ann, and Matilda, James, William and Henry, Harriet and Dorothea, came to live with their grandmother', to the very end when all seven have inexplicably disappeared into the old chest in the large spare bedroom, where they were firmly warned not to enter, for fear of solving the riddle.

The 'riddle' of where the children went puzzled readers in the same way as de la Mare's most popular poem, 'The Listeners', did. Forrest Reid was to believe it 'a dream story – a story composed or experienced in sleep. The whole thing, I take it,' he wrote, 'is simply an expression of homesickness, though the reader must discover the identity of that home in his own dreamland.' Others would find this too tenuous, and many preferred to conclude that the disappearance was symbolic of the end of childhood, a theme dear to Walter de la Mare . . . 'shades of the prison house begin to close upon the growing boy' . . . a theme equally close to Reid's heart. Sometimes, writing to his friend, as here in March 1921, one senses a note of envy:

The wonder to me is how you keep your vision so clear and unfaltering. I seem to get glimpses, but they drop away, they splutter in a series of sparks and go out. And to think that I send you all these experiments and expect you to take the will for the deed. Deep down I do so shamefacedly, though upon others I confer them with a blithe assurance. Well, good-night, F.R.

Whatever it was that he sent was corrected and returned the same month.

The corrections in your hand-writing gave them, to me, a kind of personal quality that a book cannot quite have, which is no doubt sentimentalism, but still – Also, I'm afraid the passion of the collector has been mine from the cradle. As a little boy I was forever cutting out things, and sticking in things. I collected, then, everything that could be collected; I even started a whole prep-school on the pursuit of matches – getting myself close on a hundred varieties which seems incredible. The instinct remains, though it is now limited to drawings (reproductions, alas!) and books; but it is the mere accident of impecuniosity that has imposed these limitations.

One of de la Mare's finest stories, 'Seaton's Aunt', is particularly perceptive in the character drawing of small boys and provoked the following response: 'Seaton's Aunt fills me with despair. I mean, I wish I had written it. It makes my own wretched house which I have been tinkering with seem about as romantic as one of those dreadful garden-city erections.' In mid-July 1921 Reid made a rare visit to England and spent a day with the de la Mares, writing on his return:

I am not surprised you like to talk to Colin. *I* should like to talk to him myself. I should like to have him now at the other side of the table, making drawings, running a magazine of his own, collecting something or other, interviewing me, making jokes with Arthur. Dick* rather over-awed me – particularly about H. J. – but Colin I know is exactly my contemporary, shares all my illusions, and would, in general, be a pal. He has never been to a public school, has he? It makes all the difference. Unfortunately when I next see him he will be grown-up and blasé and have discovered the Noh plays and Picasso or their future equivalents, while I am still at the stage of Huckleberry Finn . . . I really did enjoy my day with you immensely . . . Well, I hope it will come again, and till it does I have my memory of you all in your garden –

and the rabbits and the cats and the frogs and the tits eating coconuts and Miss Farjeon⁺ revealing the lost secret of Greek ballads . . . With love to everybody, Forrest Reid . . . PS Would a book about your work strike you as an idea to be dismissed without further thought? I mean, would you dislike the idea supposing it could be arranged for? Do you think such a study as the Yeats for instance, would in your case be quite too premature? I should like to do it, and I somehow feel I could do it.

The critical study was to come out eight years later, but by the close of 1921 their friendship was secure enough for Reid to feel he could offer advice and criticism. On 13 December he wrote about the short story 'The Return':

'a little child came out' . . . Why not simply 'a child'? I detest the invariable combination; it seems to me somehow 'sloppy', though no doubt this is a mere fad . . . will you forgive me if I say that your greatest danger is and always has been, in a tendency to depart from simplicity. Be as subtle as you like in your thought, but cling to simplicity of expression. In your new book of poetry for instance it seems to me that you make an excessive use of inversion – The verb comes before the noun without any other excuse than that you like it that way – a quite good excuse, I admit, but you must not let any effect freeze into a mannerism.

Early the following year he continues to argue his case:

I can't help disliking inversion even when the rhythm gains by it. I suppose what it amounts to is that I like a style that keeps as close as possible to natural speech. No poetry has a richer music than the finest poetry of Yeats and there is hardly an inversion in the whole of his work. Inversion may be used to get a particular effect of its own, but it is an effect that should be used sparingly. Once the nakedness of direct speech is abandoned, the force and depth of passionate conviction goes too. Now it is in this direction that your poetry is moving, in the direction of an increased strength and passion of actuality, and in that kind of poetry the closer you keep to natural speech the better. You cannot write poetry of this sort in the style, for instance of your 'Fairy in Winter'. I take this poem because more than any other in the book it seems to me the only chink I have ever found in your armour. I do not say that it is full of inversions. It isn't. But it is full of something that the use of inversion tends toward . . . It is pure ornament and nothing but ornament. It is written for a drawing, I know, but fairies are not the fairies of drawings and there is no fairy in your poem . . . I don't think you wrote it with the consent of anything but your hand and your pen. The dweller in you – that mysterious being – was absent when you wrote it, and he was adorably present when you wrote that other adorable winter piece, 'The Little Salamander'. I would love to talk over your new poems with you. It is so impossible to write without being far more emphatic and dogmatic than one wants to be, without being, perhaps, rather offensive. At any rate I was haunted, while I was reading, by a sense of something new, and it was this, I think, which helped to make my review so futile. I could mark in the book every line that produced in me the strange indescribable emotion of this new dawn. To put it plainly, I had a vision of a volume of poems – oh, perhaps still a long way off – that would create a world not of magic or fairies, but a world such as Traherne and Crashaw and Vaughan had glimpses of. Is this the wildest dreaming? I do not know whether a religion such as theirs, or any kind of supernatural religion, ever could mean anything to you. I do not know whether you believe in a future life for the individual, though your work is full of it.

* Colin and Dick were two of de la Mare's sons.
⁺ Eleanor Farjeon.

And it is perhaps only because your winter fairy would melt in that world like a splinter of ice in a furnace that I cavil at her whereas Miss Royde-Smith singles her out for quotation. You must forgive me. I intended to tell you a prosaic, but absolutely true ghost story which is still being enacted nightly in a house between Rosetrevor and Warrenpoint but I have already bored you sufficiently . . . Yours ever, Forrest Reid.

The drawing in question was by the American artist, Dorothy Lathrop, known and admired for her fairy illustrations. De la Mare replied to his critical friend:

I am sorry you dislike 'The Fairy in Winter' so much; simply because it gave me rather unusual pleasure to write it. Anyway, she is still there in the snow-fields of my imagination. Of course, she would melt in another climate. What I do feel is that all such beings may share one world, living their own strange lives, and yet more or less unperceived by the denizens of a different density, so to speak. We must have this all out some time. As soon as the word 'belief' is mentioned, mists begin to rise in every valley.

He also made a defence for inversion, believing it should not be attacked on principle, and he doubted 'whether ordinary talk is necessarily the best or most forcible or most attractive form of expression'. In any case Reid was to recant over inversion quite soon.

I seem to have reasoned like this: – why does this poem not move me as that other did? It is because I am conscious of an inversion in the first line. This inversion gets in my way. Now this was nonsense and I want to take it back. The truth isn't that I was not moved because there was an inversion but rather, because I was not moved, because I, in a certain case, failed in responsiveness, I became conscious of an inversion etc. The first line of 'Miss Loo' for instance, is absolutely right and without straying from your own poems I could get fifty such examples (principally to be found in *Peacock Pie*).

This exchange was in good part and provoked no rift in the friendship. Forrest Reid continued to come to England on occasion, staying with friends like E. M. Forster, Frank Workman and de la Mare. His very first visit of all had been before the First World War, not long after their St George's Cafe meeting, and he recalled this in *Private Road* in 1940.

Whether at the house in Worbeck Road or the house in Thornsett Road I have forgotten. Yet it must have been the latter, and I know John Freeman, another Georgian, lived close by. I remember the little garden at the back where clock golf was laid out on a small plot of grass. It was of this garden, I think, that the lines were written:

Breathe not – trespass not;
Of this green and darkling spot,
Latticed from the moon's beams,
Perchance a distant dreamer dreams . . .

But also, perchance I am wrong, for surely, had he been there, I should have remembered the 'little leaden lad' with which the poem ends.[5]

It is unlikely that Reid, with his discerning eye for such things, would have missed the male statue described by his friend:

While, unmoved to watch and ward,
Amid its gloomed and daisied sward
Stands with bowed and dewy head
That one little leaden lad.

This poem, 'The Sunken Garden', is cool and clear-cut, with none of the sensuality of the final pages of Reid's 'Tom Barber' trilogy.

The stone was warm. The sun had warmed the curved pouting mouth and the smooth limbs and body; but when Tom's lips pressed on those other lips the eyes were looking away from him and dimly he felt that this was a symbol of life – of life and of all love.

Stone, bronze or carved boys had appeared in at least two poems. First was W. J. Turner's 'Ecstasy' of 1919 which opens:

I saw a frieze on whitest marble drawn
Of boys who sought for shells along the shore . . .

These boys were naked and grave, their 'sweet bodies were wind-purified' and the one who 'held a shell unto his shell-like ear' had 'his eyes half-closed, his lips just breaking open'.

A few years later Humbert Wolfe's poem 'Boy in the Dusk' was published, in which the boy had parted lips and smiled 'with the broken-hearted grace of a child'. The poet asks if he is Beauty deserted, Vision betrayed, Love, or lost Youth . . .

Or he may be only
A small bronze statue
Of a boy who is lonely
And looks half at you.

'If I had never written a line . . . that would not alter my conviction that the years of childhood, boyhood and adolescence are the most significant. What follows is chiefly a logical development – the child being father of the man,' wrote Forrest Reid in 1929, and Walter de la Mare's own feelings on the importance of childhood were a strong bond in their friendship. Both genuinely liked children, enjoyed their company and their talk; de la Mare had five of his own. Both wrote of children with understanding and awareness, realising their charm, innocence, elusiveness, precocity, sometimes cruelty. Both had long been admirers of Traherne, Vaughan, and Wordsworth on the wonders and discoveries of childhood and the regret at growing older. Both quote in separate works Vaughan's

Happy those early days when I
Shined in my angel infancy.

and Wordsworth's 'Ode on the Intimations of Immortality', its poignancy reflecting their own . . .

There was a time when meadow, grove and stream,
The earth, and every common sight,
To me did seem
Apparelled in celestial light,

The glory and the freshness of a dream.
It is not now as it has been of yore; –
  Turn whereso'er I may,
  By night or day,
The things which I have seen I now can see no more . . .

Both had come under the spell of Walter Pater, and particularly his 'The Child in the House'.

The old house, as when Florian talked of it afterwards he always called it, (as all children do, who can recollect a change of home, soon enough but not too soon to mark a period in their lives) really was an old house . . . The old-fashioned, low wainscoting went round the rooms, and up the staircase with carved balusters and shadowy angles, landing half-way up at a broad window, with a swallow's nest below the sill, and the blossom of an old pear-tree showing across it in late April, against the blue, below which the perfumed juice of the find of fallen fruit in autumn was so fresh. At the next turning came the closet which held on its deep shelves the best china. Little angel faces and reedy flutings stood out round the fire-place of the children's room. And on the top of the house, above the large attic, where the white mice ran in the twilight – an infinite, unexplored wonderland of childish treasures, glass beads, empty scent-bottles, still sweet, thrum of coloured silks, among its lumber – a flat space of roof, railed round, gave a view of the neighbouring steeples; for the house, as I said, stood near a great city, which sent up heavenwards, over the twisting weather-vanes, not seldom, its beds of rolling cloud and smoke, touched with storm or sunshine. But the child of whom I am writing did not hate the fog because of the crimson lights which fell from it sometimes upon the chimneys, and the whites which gleamed through its openings, on summer mornings, on turret or pavement. For it is false to suppose that a child's sense of beauty is dependant on any choiceness or special fineness, in the objects which present themselves to it, though this indeed comes to be the rule with most of us in later life; earlier, in some degree, we see inwardly; and the child finds for itself, and with unstinted delight, a difference for the sense, in those whites and reds through the smoke on very homely buildings, and in the gold of the dandelions at the roadside, just beyond the houses, where not a handful of earth is virgin and untouched, in the lack of better ministries to its desire of beauty . . .'[6]

I quote thus at some length for the light it throws on the essential quality of Reid and de la Mare's work and on Reid's ideas for 'The Riddle'. Was this the origin for his understanding of a 'particular kind of homesickness', the inevitable time for change in the child's journey?

A letter to de la Mare on 23 December reveals:

I have had a sort of wonder book in my mind for the last few days, but whether I shall ever write it, or *could* write it, I don't know. At present it is only a wandering seed, which floated, I don't know how or why, out of a thing I have been trying to do with my own childhood. With love to you all. Yours ever, Forrest Reid.

The first glimpse of Reid's first essay in autobiography, *Apostate*[7] may have gone some way towards persuading de la Mare to work on a similar, though quite differently conceived book. Much in *Apostate* might have struck chords.

Both men had been fortunate in experiencing, in early childhood, the love and care of young women of special warmth and appeal. Reid's beloved Emma would remain vivid always. 'Emma had nursed us all, but none of the others had been exclusively her property as I was' he wrote of Emma Holmes.

And thus I seem to see, as if at the end of an immense vista, these two figures moving sedately through the sunshine, the smaller with his hands clasped behind his back, a habit he clung to even when running. He is dressed each day in a fresh blue or brown or white or even pink sailor suit, and on his head a wide-brimmed straw hat is held firmly by an elastic band that passes under his chin. Beside this figure walks, (though never holding his hand) the figure of Emma, clad in a long dark-green double-breasted coat, and carrying in one black-gloved hand a parcel of bread and in the other an umbrella.

Emma had sole care of the small Forrest at bedtimes, play-times and meal times; she told him stories and read him poetry; 'and I saw – saw while Emma read – the dark summer sea widening out and out till it melted into a golden haze that hid yet suggested an enchanted land beyond'.

When Emma left, suddenly, without saying goodbye, he found his life unbearably altered: 'a cloud, utterly impenetrable, has descended upon the hours and weeks and months and even years that followed'.

Young Jack de la Mare spent more time with his mother but was often, with his brothers and sisters, in the care of Martha Walstow from Woolwich, known as Pattie.

Pattie was the central figure in their little lives. She wore a high collar, her fuzzy hair fluffed up above it, her pretty complexion and liveliness making her seem younger than her years. Unselfish, gentle, light-hearted, to the small romantic Jack she appeared enchanting. When he became a writer his fairy stories were set in just such old-fashioned kitchens, with cakes baking, and hot bread and dripping to relish. At home, or in Hilly Fields, or by the river Ravensbourne in Forest Hill, in south-east London, Pattie would tell stories, and Jack would one day immortalize her in his poem, 'Martha':

'Once . . . once upon a time . . .'
  Over and over again,
Martha would tell us her stories,
  In the hazel glen.

Hers were those clear grey eyes
  You watch, and the story seems
Told by their beautifulness
  Tranquil as dreams.

She'd sit with her two slim hands
  Clasped round her bended knees;
While we on our elbows lolled,
  And stared at ease.

Her voice and her narrow chin,
  Her grave small lovely head,
Seemed half the meaning
  Of the words she said.

'Once . . . once upon a time . . .'
   Like a dream you dream in the night,
Fairies and gnomes stole out
   In the leaf-green light.

And her beauty far away
   Would fade, as her voice ran on,
Till hazel and summer sun
   And all were gone:

All fordone and forgot;
   And like clouds in the height of the sky,
Our hearts stood still in the hush
   Of an age gone by.

Reid continued to suggest that de la Mare should contain his memories in autobiographical form, but when *Early One Morning in Spring* came out in 1935 it was not an autobiography but a large, wide-ranging anthology covering every aspect of childhood.[8] At times the editor reveals himself and his own children; his intention was to retrieve his childhood through the memories and accounts of others. It is an entirely unique collection. There are altogether eleven quotations from *Apostate* under the book's headings of 'Woes', 'Night-Fears', 'Solitude' and 'Stories'. In this last de la Mare quotes the passage about Reid's recurring childhood dream and traces it, as Reid himself does, up to the time of his attempt to recapture the experience in a story . . . which, on rereading, displeased him: 'My fairy gold was trash,' wrote Reid. 'This was the story I had written, but it was not the story I had tried to write.'

'And what in essence,' answers de la Mare, 'is that strange and memorable novel *Uncle Stephen*, but an attempt to capture this early dream . . . and all imaginations, all really creative ideas, are something akin to dreams.'

Reid tells us in *Private Road* that he and WJ – the term by which many of his friends addressed him – often talked of ghosts, haunted houses and dreams, and even a cursory glance through de la Mare's poems lights on these themes, along with shadows and elf-like faces in the windows of deserted houses . . .

Nothing on the grey roof, nothing on the brown,
Only a little greening where the rain drips down;
Nobody at the window, nobody at the door,
Only a little hollow which a foot once wore;
But still I tread on tiptoe, still tiptoe on I go,
Past nettles, porch and weedy well, for oh, I know
A friendless face is peering, and a still clear eye
Peeps closely through the casement as my step goes by.
      (The Old Stone House)

To return briefly to *Early One Morning*. In the section on 'Dolls, Toys & Play' de la Mare refers to the boy Reid's discovery of the pile of magazines in the attic, and concludes: 'Scissors, candlelight and musty murk – that afternoon a craving sprang up in his heart; and for proof of its ravages there is his packed and absorbing *Illustrators*

of the Sixties.' And amongst those thanked under acknowledgments is 'My friend, Mr Forrest Reid, not only for many quotations from *Apostate* but for his great kindness in reading nearly the whole of my proofs'. The introduction to another book, a collection of essays and articles, *Pleasures and Speculations* (1940) ends: 'Finally my old friend Mr Forrest Reid has read through my revised page proofs. They alone could reveal my debt to him. This is the latest (but I hope not the last) of many similar kindnesses – Again and again, so to speak we have shared the same ink-pot . . .'[9]

In his 1953 biography of Forrest Reid,[10] Russell Burlingham mentions that in Reid's inscribed copy of de la Mare's story for children, 'The Lord Fish', is written:

To FR from WJ
Once were two friends whose livelong wish
Was in a sea of ink to fish:
   By hook and crook –
   By crook and hook,
They now and then hauled up a Book.
See! here's another: Look!

De la Mare also dedicated his selection of short stories, *On the Edge*, to Reid, and wrote the introduction to Burlingham's biography, which being out of print is worth quoting almost in its entirety.

As any reader of this book will at once discover there was not the least need for any word in it by way of an introduction. This, however, does not make it any less of the special pleasure it is to me to have the opportunity of saying how sure I feel that Forrest Reid would himself have greatly valued and delighted in it. And how could that be otherwise? It has qualities not only after his own heart but such as he abundantly shared – insight, understanding, sagacity, courage, candour, enthusiasm and a true affection. And every page of it is clearly the outcome of a most scrupulous care. Nor does this in the least strain Mr. Burlingham's own declaration on page 18 that Forrest Reid could 'never be roped in, no lasso was ever long enough'! I see again, as I read these words, that slow, familiar, mischievous smile stealing over his face – the long upper lip, the restless eyebrows, the slanting glance from those greenish, scrutinizing, unfaltering eyes.

He was in everything that he cared for most (and he cared for much) an unflagging devotee – from old woodcuts to Championship croquet, to street cricket, bull-dogs, story-technique, and, via Wagner, to Italian Opera. He exulted in the rigour of the game, whether it was Bridge or prosody. In the work of others, as, within its chosen range, of his own, he was a zealot – an eager and therefore exacting zealot. He loved this earthly life, and no less fully and fervently that of the imagination and the spirit. All this is explored and made clear in the pages that follow. And, no less, how devotedly he loved his friends, and they him; and how honestly and openly he detested – what he detested. That many of them should have recently expressed their affection and admiration 'over the air' would have delighted him. That Mr. Burlingham has still, in Time, so far to journey, and, in ink, will then so much achieve, before even middle-age comes within view, would have been no less a joy to him. For 'F.R.' that battered abstraction, 'the younger generation', cast no shadow of disquietude; nor, I am sure, had he any relish for the philanthropic phrase, 'juvenile delinquent'. You had to take him or leave him as he was in himself; he could no other. Endlessly active, he was yet a Dreamer; unflinchingly matter-of-fact, he had drunk 'the milk of Paradise'; and the Greek Anthology was in his bones. The belief he blessed most was the belief in goodness; and nothing could be more sovranly typical of his most generous simplicity than the last few words of the first letter, clean out of the bluest blue, that, on 1 June, 1912, he wrote to me, mentioning that he had reviewed one of my books:

'I do not suppose you take much interest in such things, but if you should gather from them that I wish you well . . . that is all I desire.'

And so it always was, throughout an unbroken friendship of half my long lifetime: an inexhaustible patience (sadly needed); wise counsel; life-giving encouragement; a selfless sharing of all he cared for most. As for labour for love; for years and years we 'took in' one another's proofs: his a model, mine a sort of literary mince-meat. He never spared *any* pains, his counsel was beyond price.

No wonder, then, this book rejoices me beyond words. No longer will Edwin Muir's recent tribute and lament *both* hold good concerning this 'true artist' – that 'his genius has never been adequately examined'. And once discerned and established in the minds of those possessing even a grain of it themselves, the roots of genius pierce deep, and its fruit never fails.

Forrest Reid's finest tribute to Walter de la Mare must be the 1929 critical study, also long out of print, though still of interest to students of literature. All areas of de la Mare's vast output are considered, and the scholarship is sound and appreciative without over-praise. As always Reid proves himself a discerning critic.

Reid's two biographers, Russell Burlingham and Brian Taylor, confessed difficulty in assessing him, and this was immensely reassuring to me. This story of a friendship between two interesting and highly individual writers needs further research. I hope in time to study more of their long correspondence, and almost look on what I have written so far as a preliminary treatment. Perhaps, by then, there will be a much-needed revival of interest in Reid's books, particularly *Apostate*, and perhaps a more perceptive critic will dispel Peter Coveney's narrow-minded assessment of him in *The Image of Childhood* (1967) when he pronounced: 'The unacceptability of the emotional realities of his theme was in large measure responsible for creating the idealizing dishonesty of this kind of literature.' Perhaps, by then, Walter de la Mare will have the recognition he is owed, as poet, as one of the finest editors of all time, and as one of the masters of the short story.

Forrest Reid, well aware of this back in the early twenties wrote to him on 23 March 1922 saying:

I was overjoyed to get your letter and your stories. I don't know how it is but these prose tales of yours seem especially written for me. At any rate no other stories produce upon me the same effect. I don't seem to read them but they seem to happen to me. With the first sentence I forget everything but what is happening, and with the last I come back to my everyday senses with a sudden bump and a slightly dazed feeling and things are not just the same when I do come back . . . Publish them all and place them in chronological order and date them. This will add immensely to the interest of the whole collection. And I know you won't do it. When the time comes you'll leave out half of them and some of my favourites. And it won't be the least use, from your point of view, because when we're both dust and ashes they're bound to be printed by somebody without the advantage of any little verbal changes you might want to make . . .

Giles de la Mare, the writer's publisher grandson, brought out Volume One of the short stories at the end of 1996.[11]

Notes

1. Forrest Reid, *Walter de la Mare, a critical study*, London: Faber & Faber, 1929.
2. Selections from the letters of Forrest Reid to Walter de la Mare are from the correspondence in the Bodleian Library, Oxford. I have not discovered the whereabouts of de la Mare's letters to Reid, and all extracts from correspondence and literary quotations are taken from Theresa Whistler's biography of de la Mare, *Imagination of the Heart* (Duckworth, 1993), from which I have also taken Naomi Royde Smith's description of Walter de la Mare.
3. *The Collected Poems of Walter de la Mare*, London: Faber & Faber, 1969.
4. Walter de la Mare, *The Riddle and other stories*, London: Faber & Faber, 1923.
5. Forrest Reid, *Private Road*, London: Faber & Faber, 1940.
6. Walter Pater, *Studies in the History of the Renaissance*, London and New York: Macmillan, 1873.
7. Forrest Reid, *Apostate*, London: Constable, 1926, reprinted Faber & Faber, 1947.
8. Walter de la Mare (ed.), *Early One Morning. An anthology on childhood*, London: Faber & Faber, 1935.
9. Walter de la Mare, *Pleasures and Speculations*, London: Faber & Faber, 1940.
10. Russell Burlingham, *Forrest Reid*, London: Faber & Faber, 1953.
11. *The collected short stories of Walter de la Mare*, Vol. 1, Giles de la Mare, 1996. (Vols 2 and 3 are to follow.)

9   Tomorrow Evening about Eight

Robert Greacen

I came back from school, where I was in my last year, and put my bike away in the shed in the back yard. It was a bright, mild June day, almost cloudless in a way we seldom experienced in the north, where the low clouds – so low that one could nearly stand on a ladder and touch them – hardly ever disappeared. The school day had been like most school days, mildly boring, slightly tiresome. I was nearing the end of my school career. I had started, I hoped not too late, to make an effort in Maths and Physics but without any real interest in the subjects. I was rapidly developing a passion, an obsession for something else. Mother came in briskly from the shop.

'I'm glad you're back, Robbie. There's a telegram for you.'

'A what?' I said, 'Who would send me a telegram?'

'Well,' said mother, 'I hope it's nothing to do with politics. Politics only gets people into trouble. You just mind your lessons and leave politics to them that has nothing better to do.'

'Cut out the speeches, mother,' I said. 'You're not on a soap box down at the Custom House steps. I'm not either – not yet! Now where's the telegram?'

She fished it out from behind Granny McCrea's photo on the mantelpiece. I noticed my surname was misspelt – as usual. I ripped it open and read: COME TOMORROW EVENING ABOUT EIGHT STOP FORREST REID.

I jumped in the air – or at least I think I did. Then I hugged mother fiercely.

'You're very affectionate today,' she said, smiling.

'I've only one problem,' I said. 'I can't decide whether to be the next socialist Prime Minister or the Poet Laureate.'

'What a lot of fool talk,' she said, though still looking pleased. 'I don't know where you get all these strange ideas. It isn't from my side of the family. We're all sane.'

The implication was that some of father's relatives were not.

I showed her the telegram. 'I've never heard of this Mr Reid. I hope he's respectable and goes to church on a Sunday?'

'Respectable,' I said with contempt. 'The man is famous everywhere except in his native city, that is. He certainly isn't a *petit bourgeois*.'

'You may know a wee bit of French,' said mother, 'but that doesn't mean you have an iota of sense. Anyway, I hope this Mr Reid isn't a Sinn Feiner or a communist.'

'He's apolitical,' I said. 'He's a man who writes books.'

'Well,' admitted mother, 'that's not as bad as I thought, but I've heard it said that these writer fellows are hardly ever sober. Now if he offers you alcohol, refuse it.'

I was in a daze. A telegram, no less! An invitation from a famous writer! Though I never had much of a voice for singing I burst into song:

You've heard of General Wellington, who won at Waterloo,
But there's a good old Irishman I'll mention unto you,
He comes from dear old Dublin, he's a man we all applaud,
For he always finds a corkscrew more handy than the sword.
He's good old General Guinness, he's a soldier strong and 'stout'
Found on every 'bottle-front' and he can't be done without.
His noble name has world-wide fame, for every heart he cheers,
Good old General Guinness of the Dublin 'booseliers'.

'I wonder what your headmaster, Mr Henderson, would say if he saw you now,' said mother, laughing.

'My dear old headmaster, Mr Henderson,' I replied, 'wouldn't touch Guinness with a Lagan barge pole. Nothing for him – good Scotsman that he is – but the finest Scotch malt.'

When I had been at the elementary school, we were asked to write an occasional composition. To my surprise, this was the easiest bit of work we were ever given – so much easier than the tiresome columns of long addition sums, as if anyone other than grocers really cared what they added up to, anyway. I delighted in words and tried to learn new ones, long ones, strange ones, rich and rare ones. I marvelled at the effect words had on others. Short, vulgar or obscene ones had an enormous effect as when someone called a boy a 'bastard' or 'wee skitter' or chalked the word 'fuck' on the wall of a urinal. Long, learned ones, like 'exasperation', drew exclamations of surprise, even pleasure, from the dour taskmasters who were our teachers.

A master once handed me back a composition and said, 'You write like Dickens.' From that moment I determined to be a writer in addition to whatever else I should become. For all I knew, the master was merely indulging in sarcasm. The speaker was either a Mr Harbinson or a Mr McCullough (the latter being the dark, sardonic vice-principal of the school). The face and name have vanished, the words remain. *Words, words, words* – how they could charm away the devils of fear and depression, especially when they were printed words.

Belfast, unlike Dublin, could hardly be called a city of wits and poets, though indeed we had a few dedicated spirits. The hand of Protestantism had grasped our community firmly and made it worthy if not virtuous, hard-working and thrifty. The 'Black Man' statue outside the grammar school, the Academical Institution, known popularly as 'Inst.', symbolised the Victorian attitudes that, in the 1930s, still prevailed. (The statue, still there, is of an eminent divine, Dr Henry Cooke, and has been darkened by the elements – hence the name given it.)

As I say, despite the inhospitable atmosphere, a few writers had managed to survive. There was Robert Lynd, the gentle essayist and convert to home rule, whose father had been minister at May Street Presbyterian Church. Lynd had found success in London. Rumour had it that he was a hard drinker who once said to a fellow-boozer in a Fleet Street tavern, 'Do you realise that we are the kind of men our mothers warned us against?' My mother, simple soul though she was, had a point and I knew it.

Forrest Reid, then, was *the* literary artist living amongst us: a novelist and autobiographer who wrote for a minority, something perhaps of a cult figure. Sometimes, after the final ring of the school bell, I used to ride off on my bike to Smithfield – now long gone – to browse among the second-hand books in Hugh Greer's and rummage in the fourpenny and sixpenny boxes. It was there by some lucky chance or, more realistically, by a process of seeking and therefore finding, that I came across Forrest Reid's *Apostate* in which he looks back on his childhood and youth. I read these words:

Sunday became to me a veritable nightmare, casting its baleful shadow even over the last hours of Saturday. I hated Sunday, I hated church, I hated Sunday School, I hated Bible stories, I hated everybody mentioned in both the Old and New Testaments, except perhaps the impenitent thief, Eve's snake, and a few similar characters. And I never disguised these feelings. From dawn till sunset the day of rest was for me a day of storm and battle, renewed each week, and carried on for years with a pertinacity that now seems hardly credible till at length the opposition was exhausted and I was allowed to go my own way.

This, indeed, was a soul speaking unto a kindred soul. I, too, had waged such a battle, and I too, in the end, had been allowed to go my own way. The street corner evangelists would have consigned me to the flames of hell as readily as they would any Papist. I, who had been granted the opportunity to know better! At last I knew that in rebelliousness there had been at least one forerunner, a member of the writing tribe.

How thrilling it was to discover a writer whose pages had inprinted on them familiar names such as Mount Charles, the University Road and the Botanic Gardens, for it was precisely this area of Belfast, the immediate vicinity of my grammar school, for which I had the deepest affection. I turned the pages of *Apostate*, lost in a reverie of delight as paragraph after paragraph spoke to me.

This one, for instance:

There was the beauty of an autumn afternoon in the Ormeau Park at dusk, when, with the dead leaves thick on the deserted paths, I had sat listening to a German band playing somewhere out of sight of the railings. Through the twilight, with its yellow twinkling of street lamps, the music had floated. The tune was the old *Lorelei*, but into the plaintive twang of those instruments all the melancholy of the earth had passed. It was as if the very soul of the empty park had found a voice, and were sobbing out its complaint to the November sky.

The assistant in Greer's came up and gave me a hard look. 'You've been readin' that wee book a quare long time,' he said. 'It's gettin' on for closin' time. Are you thinkin' of buyin' it?'

'Yes,' I said.

In this way, a new name came into my consciousness. Forrest Reid, one of my teachers told me, still lived in Belfast, out at Knock, he believed. Up to that time, I thought all writers lived in London or perhaps down south in Dublin. The teacher also told me that Reid had once gone out to a local shop in his pyjamas – such was the daftness of writers. With all speed, I ransacked the Public Library in Royal Avenue for Reid's other books, the novels *Uncle Stephen*, *Brian Westby* and *Following Darkness* (the last renamed *Peter Waring*) and read them avidly.

But the novels, unlike *Apostate*, disappointed me. They seemed, for all their lyrical charm and their fastidious sentence construction, to be too limited. Nobody I had read so far had written so sensitively of childhood and, more particularly, boyhood, but, outside the magic years of adolescence, Forrest Reid seemed to be at a loss. His adults did not ring true. At the time I sensed this but did not know why, for homosexuality was something I knew nothing about, not even the word itself. And yet, I had to admit that for me Reid was one of the great men – the only great man, perhaps – living in our matter-of-fact and all too philistine city.

I looked Reid up in *Who's Who* in the Central Library. Reid had been educated at Inst. and Cambridge. The university in Belfast had conferred an honorary doctorate on him. He was a keen croquet player. Like our city, I was matter-of-fact on one point. I wanted his address and there it was in *Who's Who*: 13 Ormiston Crescent. Having lately acquired a Remington portable typewriter, second-hand at five pounds, I typed out, as best I could, several of my poems and a short story, and wrote a letter that started:

Dear Mr Reid,
I having read much of your work with admiration, I a schoolboy with the ambition to become a writer, am taking the liberty of sending you some examples of my poetry and fiction.

Forrest Reid replied, in a remarkably neat hand, to the effect that he had read my manuscripts with interest and that they showed 'promise'. Would I like to call on him some evening so that he could discuss them with me? I replied that any evening would suit me fine. Hence the telegram.

On that memorable Tuesday evening, within a minute or two of eight, I reached Ormiston Crescent. I got off my Raleigh sports bike and walked gingerly past No. 13. He had said 'about eight' so I walked to the end of the street and then back again to the pebble-dashed little house that was No. 13. In my naivety, I had supposed that a famous novelist would live in a large house with a long drive up to the front door. There one would ring the bell and be admitted by a butler straight out of P. G. Wodehouse. 'What name shall I give, sir?' he would enquire in BBC announcer tones. Then I would be ushered into the study where the novelist himself, in evening dress, would be clutching an extremely dry martini. He would offer me one and I would refuse politely, explaining that I had a sore throat. But here he was in a house smaller than the one inhabited by my non-famous Uncle Johnny in Edgbaston – Uncle Johnny who had left school at fourteen and now sliced bacon and weighed out tea for a living. Life was full of surprises.

I rang the bell. Instead of a butler in tails, out came Forrest Reid himself. A man in casual tweeds, he held a pipe awkwardly and peered at me through thick-lensed glasses as if he were a sensitive, easily-frightened animal.

'Come in,' he said, politely.

In I went to make the acquaintance of the most famous man in Belfast.

He thanked me for letting him see my work and he talked about it. Yes, definitely promising but rather derivative. Didn't I think so myself? What writers had I been reading? Did I know the poetry of his friend de la Mare? Had I read Yeats? I muttered something about liking *Innisfree* and he smiled. Had I said something wrong? I mentioned Swinburne and then proceeded to quote Tennyson. He corrected me gently and I could have bitten my tongue. Literature, he told me, needed work . . . concentration . . . dedication.

I said I was a socialist. He replied that politics did not interest him. Politicians were loud people, vulgar, often insincere. The European situation was menacing. He said he loathed the Germans and their abominable Fuhrer, who couldn't even speak German properly, and that – apart from Goethe – German writers of note had all been

Jews. The room in which this conversation took place contained more books than I had ever seen in a private house. How was it possible for a man to gather, let alone read, so many? He made tea which we drank out of delicate china. No wine, whiskey or martinis were offered, so I was spared the embarrassment of refusal. 'Come again,' he said kindly, 'and do send me some more of your poems and stories.'

So it was that my first writer turned out to be avuncular and intelligent, but unlike any of my real uncles. As I rode home, I felt that somehow they were, in their rough, homespun way, more real as people, more manly. Forrest Reid was what? A private man, yes, a private man who allowed only a few to cross the threshold into his interior world. Belfast knew him not and he had no wish to know Belfast. But what had I expected from him? Some kind of lightning flash that would illuminate the whole of life? The boy who rode away from Ormiston Crescent was a somewhat different one from the boy who arrived with glowing face and high hopes on a close June evening.

True, I went back two or three times to the little house, and its book-lined study always fascinated me. Perhaps I warmed to Reid's vast assembly of books more than I warmed to Reid himself. He seemed to be hiding away in a world beyond my reach. In later years, we exchanged a few letters and he kindly contributed to a couple of anthologies I edited. He sent me a warm note of congratulation on my marriage, an institution, I imagine, for which he had scant regard. But soon after these visits I found new literary gods. One of these was the Viking god reincarnated as Wystan Hugh Auden.

Yet all these years after meeting Forrest Reid, I find pleasure in recalling that I knew, however slightly, the author of *Apostate*. Nor do I forget that the young Reid once saw Oscar Wilde – an unlikely figure among the linen merchants and the shipyard workers of Belfast – climb up and sit beside the coachman on the box seat of a carriage. Culpable escapism no doubt, but I cannot help longing in this noisy, polluted age for the placid days of Forrest Reid's boyhood when the Linen Hall still existed and the inner suburbs were almost rural and 'the few horse trams, their destination indicated by the colour of their curtains, did little to disturb the quiet of the streets'.

10

Catalogue
Paul Goldman

The arrangement of the entries in this catalogue relates to the chapters in Reid's book *Illustrators of the Eighteen Sixties* (henceforth referred to as *Illustrators*) published by Faber and Gwyer in 1928 and reprinted in 1975 by Dover Publications. His discussion of individual artists begins in Chapter 3 and continues between Chapters 5 and 14. Reid's grouping of the artists remains intact although modern scholarship might differ with him as to who, for example, should be classified as a 'Pre-Raphaelite' or a member of the 'Idyllic' school. I have attempted to convey, as far as possible, Reid's enthusiasms as they are reflected both in the collection at Oxford and in his writing.

Since almost all the works were removed by Reid from periodicals, the measurements are to the image, with height preceding width as is customary. For certain periodicals, notably *Good Words*, I have been unable to provide the month of publication. This is because such details were contained on the fragile paper wrappers of the single issues and almost never survived the knife when prepared for binding in the yearly volumes.

Chapter 3
Some Precursors

Here Reid deals with the work of John Gilbert, Birket Foster and John Tenniel. Since the Ashmolean collection contains almost nothing by Foster he is omitted here. Reid wrote of these artists that they 'remained uninfluenced either by the Pre-Raphaelites or the school of naturalistic artists that succeeded them ...' (*Illustrators,* p.20).

1. John Gilbert (1817–1897)
The Suit of Armour
Wood-engraving by Joseph Swain.
174 × 116 mm

In *Once a Week*, 24 November 1866, although intended as the frontispiece for the July to December 1866 volume of the magazine. This design does not seem to relate to any particular text in the issue of 24 November. Reproduced by Reid facing p.21.

Reid recognised that Gilbert's most important ventures were probably his edition of Longfellow of 1856 and some eight hundred drawings the artist made for a complete edition of Shakespeare. This enormous publication by Routledge appeared in parts between 1856 and 1858 and was later produced as a three-volume set.

2. John Tenniel (1820–1914)
The Norse Princess
Wood-engraving by the Dalziel Brothers.
185 × 114 mm

In *Good Words*, 1863, facing p.201.
Reid wrote of Tenniel 'It is on his designs for the two *Alices*, however, that Tenniel's fame as an illustrator rests. Never was a text more completely grasped, expanded, and illuminated.' (*Illustrators,* p.28).

The poem is by Alexander Smith.

And upward to a sea-o'er-staring peak
With lamentation was the princess borne
And, looking northward, left with evening meek
And fiery-bosomed morn.

1.   John Gilbert, *The Suit of Armour*

Chapter 5
The Pre-Raphaelite Group

Reid included in this chapter Rossetti, Hunt, Brown, M. J. Lawless, Sandys, Millais, Hughes, Poynter, Burne-Jones, Simeon Solomon and H. H. Armstead. Unfortunately, there is nothing in the collection by Rossetti at all and no important designs by Brown and hence both artists are omitted here.

3. William Holman Hunt (1827–1910)
At Night
Wood-engraving by Joseph Swain.
78 × 127 mm

In *Once a Week*, 21 July 1860, p.102. Reproduced by Reid facing p.46 in an impression showing Hunt's instructions to the engraver.

Although Reid compared Hunt's work unfavourably with that of Rossetti, remarking that it was 'less imaginative, less lyrical in quality', he concluded that 'it is always distinguished' (*Illustrators*, p.47).

The final verse of the unattributed poem reads:

'*O, what is this sudden pang?*
Is it growing darker, Will?
Heavily goes my heart, –
It is almost standing still!
Raise me – I cannot breathe –
Pray for me, love,' she said.
'*Father, into* Thy *hands!'*
And my young wife was dead.

4. William Holman Hunt

Lost
Steel-engraving by Joseph Brown.
133 × 83 mm

Frontispiece to Dinah Mulock (Mrs Craik), *Studies from Life*, 1862, published in Hurst and Blackett's *Standard Library*.

Reid wrote: 'The drawing is a miracle of minute detail, but, perhaps because of the smooth hard impersonal character it shares with all steel engravings, contains nothing by which one could identify the artist were his name not printed below it.' (*Illustrators*, p.48).

5. Matthew James Lawless (1837–1864)

The Head Master's Sister
Wood-engraving by Joseph Swain.
99 × 125 mm

In *Once a Week*, 28 April 1860, p.389.

Reid wrote of Lawless that he 'had individuality, and, though he was faithful to the Pre-Raphaelite tradition, his drawings are stamped with a personal note that makes them as easy to identify as those of that very different artist, Charles Keene. Whether he would ever have developed into a great draughtsman it is impossible to say. At his death he had not yet done so ... But he is always interesting, always sincere, ...' (*Illustrators*, p.51).

The story by Herbert Vaughan (pseudonym of Vaughan Morgan) concerns the love between Frank Ainslie and the head master's sister Clara Martin. The two are finally united after he returns from India, having been wounded but now a holder of the Victoria Cross. However, Lawless illustrates an earlier point in the narrative: 'And they were ferried across the little stream; and when Clara saw the promised picture, she owned it could not be praised too highly.'

5.   Matthew James Lawless, *The Head Master's Sister*

4.   William Holman Hunt, *Lost*

6. Matthew James Lawless

One Dead
Wood-engraving by Walter Barker.
101 × 126 mm

In *Churchman's Family Magazine*, September 1863, facing p.75. Dated 1862 in the block.

Reid simply called this design 'a masterpiece' (*Illustrators*, p.52) and reproduced it on p.54.

The opening verse of this anonymous poem reads:

Traffic meets traffic in the thronging streets;
Friendship greets friendship; love to love is wed;
Grief keepeth house within a childless home
Whence one hath joined the dead.

7. Frederick Sandys (1832–1904)

The Sailor's Bride
Wood-engraving by Joseph Swain.
85 × 125 mm

In *Once a Week*, 13 April 1861, p.434. Reproduced by Reid on p.9. He stated that the original block which had been engraved by W. H. Hooper was rejected by Sandys and then engraved by Swain (*Illustrators*, p.xiii).

Reid wrote: 'Though Sandys lived for more than seventy years his twenty-five drawings for the wood were all made well within our period, and they rank among the most important it produced.' (*Illustrators*, p.55). Of this particular design he remarked that it is 'a lovely thing, revealing more tenderness than he usually displays' (p.59).

The poem by Marian James concerns a woman who dies before she can marry her sailor lover. One verse reads:

Then stole a cloud across her face;
'All things are growing dim,
Mother! Can this be death? Kiss me,
And give my love to him.'

9. Frederick Sandys, *Rosamond, Queen of the Lombards*

8. Frederick Sandys

Harald Harfagr
Wood-engraving by Joseph Swain.
184 × 108 mm

In *Once a Week*, 2 August 1862, p.154.

The poem by George Borrow 'purposes to be a dialogue between a Valkyrie, or chooser of the slain, and a Raven, and gives a graphic account of Harald's wars and domestic matters'. The first verse reads:

Ye men wearing bracelets
Be mute whilst I sing
Of Harald the hero –
High Norroway's king;
I'll duly declare
A discourse I heard
Betwixt a bright maiden
And black raven bird.

9. Frederick Sandys

Rosamond, Queen of the Lombards
Wood-engraving by Joseph Swain.
129 × 115 mm

In *Once a Week*, 30 November 1861. Reproduced by Reid on p.57.

Reid wrote of this drawing that it 'is among the supreme designs of the Pre-Raphaelite school, and indeed of the whole black and white art of England … Its melody of line, its richness and imaginative power, place this drawing very high even among Sandys's best things' (*Illustrators*, p.59).

The relevant verse of the poem which is signed CJE or perhaps CSE reads:

She raised the scull-cup to her lips,
Queenlike she gazed around,
Across her heart a shadow slips –
'Ah me! how sharp the memory grips
Of wild Lord Cunimond!'

10. Frederick Sandys

The Old Chartist
Wood-engraving by Joseph Swain.
105 × 127 mm

In *Once a Week*, 8 February 1862, p.183.
Reproduced by Reid on p.61.

   Reid remarked: 'The subject here is taken
neither from legend nor from the past, the old
Chartist of George Meredith's poem is simply an
English working man, leaning in meditation
over a bridge, beneath which a brook flows
through a woody landscape' (*Illustrators*, p.59).

> *Well, well! Not beaten – spite of them, I shout;*
> *And my estate is suffering for the Cause. –*
> *Now, what is yon brown water-rat about,*
> *Who washes his old poll with busy paws?*
>   *What does he mean by't?*
> *It's like defying all our natural laws,*
> *For him to hope that he'll get clean by't.*

11. Frederick Sandys

The Waiting Time
Wood-engraving by W.Thomas.
177 × 115 mm

In *Churchman's Family Magazine*, 1863, facing
p.91. Reproduced by Reid on p.62.

   The poem by Sarah Doudney is entitled 'The
Hardest Time of all' and is concerned with the
poverty and hardship suffered by the weavers in
Lancashire when the American Civil War
prevented supplies of raw cotton reaching the
mills in the north of England. The poem opens
as follows:

> *There are days of deepest sorrow*
> *In the season of our life;*
> *There are wild, despairing moments,*
> *There are hours of mental strife.*
> *There are times of stony anguish,*
> *When the tears refuse to fall;*
> *But the waiting time, my brothers,*
> *Is the hardest time of all.*

11.   Frederick Sandys, *The Waiting Time*

12. Frederick Sandys

If

Wood-engraving by Joseph Swain.

159 × 114 mm.

In the *Argosy*, March 1866, facing p.336.

The poem is by Christina Rossetti, and the woman yearns for her lover who is 'miles and miles away from me across the sea'. The fourth verse reads as follows:

In this weary world it is so cold, so cold,
While I sit here all alone;
I would not like to wait and to grow old,
But just to be dead and gone.

" If he would come to-day, to-day,
O, what a day to-day would be !"

12.   Frederick Sandys, *If*

13. John Everett Millais (1829–1896)

The Lost Piece of Silver
Wood-engraving by the Dalziel Brothers.
140 × 109 mm

In *Good Words*, 1863, facing p.605. Reproduced
by Reid on p.65. In the magazine the text was
'read in the light of the present day by Thomas
Guthrie D.D.'. Guthrie (1803–1873) was a Free
Church minister and from 1864 until his death
editor of *The Sunday Magazine*.

Reid called *The Parables of Our Lord*
Millais's 'masterpiece' and continued, 'Of this
superb work much has been written but it is
worthy of all the praise ever bestowed upon it.
Here we have the artist determined to do his
best, sparing himself no pains, making as
elaborate studies for his designs as Rossetti or
Sandys did for theirs.' (*Illustrators*, pp.71-2).
Later (p.75) he pointed out that '"The Lost
Piece of Silver" is in pattern the most simple of
all the drawings. The line has the flowing elastic
quality of a water weed streaming in a current.'

Millais made twenty drawings for the
Parables, the first twelve of which appeared in
Good Words in 1863. The entire set appeared in
book form in 1864.

14. John Everett Millais

The Prodigal Son
Wood-engraving by the Dalziel Brothers.
139 × 109 mm

In *Good Words*, 1863, facing p.161.
Reid wrote: '"The Prodigal Son" is among
the finest drawings of all. The pattern of the
pagoda-like hut at the top of the picture is
repeated in the exquisitely drawn cedar-trees:
the contrasting tones are rich and full of colour.'
(*Illustrators*, pp.75-6).

13.   John Everett Millais, *The Lost Piece of Silver*

15. John Everett Millais

The Good Samaritan
Wood-engraving by the Dalziel Brothers.
141 × 109 mm

In *Good Words,* 1863, facing p.241.
   Reid appreciates in this design its 'dramatic power and beauty of composition' (*Illustrators,* p.75).

15.   John Everett Millais, *The Good Samaritan*

16. John Everett Millais
The Wise and Foolish Virgins
Wood-engraving by the Dalziel Brothers.
139 × 108 mm

In *Good Words*, 1863, facing p.81.

17. John Everett Millais
Son Christopher
Wood-engraving by Joseph Swain.
102 × 127 mm

In *Once a Week*, 31 October 1863, p.519.
Reproduced by Reid facing p.80.

    The story by Harriet Martineau, which was
described in the magazine as 'An Historiette', is
set in Lyme Regis in the year 1685 and is
concerned with the rebellion of Monmouth.
Millais provided eight illustrations to the work
which was serialised between 24 October and 12
December 1863. Reid remarked 'how infinitely
more charming is the boy … as he sits buried in
his book, for the reason that he is not prettified
and idealized' (*Illustrators,* p.80).

18. John Everett Millais
Death Dealing Arrows
Wood-engraving by the Dalziel Brothers.
139 × 88 mm

In *Once a Week*, 25 January 1868, p.79.
    Unusually, this appears to be an
independent design with no relationship to any
particular text.

16.   John Everett Millais, *The Wise and Foolish Virgins*

THE LAST DAYS OF BARRY LYNDON.

19.   John Everett Millais, *The Last Days of Barry Lyndon*

19. John Everett Millais
The Last Days of Barry Lyndon
Wood-engraving by Joseph Swain.
133 × 100 mm

In W. M. Thackeray, *The Memoirs of Barry
Lyndon*, Smith, Elder collected edition of
Thackeray's works, Vol. xix, 1879.
   Reid wrote: 'we have the four admirable
illustrations made for Thackeray's *Barry
Lyndon* (1879), one of which at least, "The Last
Days", is a masterpiece. The drawing of that
drunken figure seated at the table is the most
realistic and the most terrible design Millais
ever made.' (*Illustrators,* p.79).

20. Arthur Hughes (1832–1915)
Blessing in Disguise
Wood-engraving by the Dalziel Brothers.
150 × 124 mm

In *The Sunday Magazine*, 1 December 1868,
p.156.
   Reid recognised that Hughes 'had what is
rarer than clever draughtsmanship, a spark of
genius, and a personal charm so persuasive that
it goes far to make up for a somewhat wobbly
technique'. He saw the present design as 'among
his most beautiful designs' (*Illustrators,* p.84).
   Hughes was particularly admired for his
work in the periodical *Good Words for the Young*
where among other things he memorably
illustrated George Macdonald's *At The Back of
the North Wind*. Unfortunately none of these
illustrations is to be found in the collection at
Oxford.
   The first verse of the poem, which is simply
signed with the initial 'M', reads:

   Mine eyes were stiffened with the last night's tears
   And my brow ached too heavily to weep,
   Opprest with sorrow past and future fears,
   Too weary to awake – too sad to sleep.

20.   Arthur Hughes, *Blessing in Disguise*

"THE DIAL."

21. Arthur Hughes, *The Dial*

21. Arthur Hughes
The Dial
Wood-engraving by an unidentified engraver.
187 × 127 mm

In *Good Words*, 1871, facing p.183.
    The poem is by F.W. Simmons and the thirteenth verse reads:

> *She pluckt a rose with tender care;*
> *Brooding she panted o'er the flower:*
> *The sunlight toucht her golden hair,*
> *And mark'd the hour.*

22. Edward John Poynter (1836–1919)
A Dream of Love
Wood-engraving by Joseph Swain.
126 × 112 mm

In *Once a Week*, 4 October 1862, p.393.
    Reid did not think highly of Poynter as an illustrator and dismissed him somewhat cursorily as 'not among our most interesting illustrators' (*Illustrators*, p.95). However, he recognised that Poynter went through a vaguely Pre-Raphaelite phase, especially with this drawing.
    The story, in two parts, concerns Amyce Cloyse and her great-uncle, Sir John Cloyse who had adopted her as a child on the death of her parents in India.

23. Edward John Poynter
The Kissing Bush
Wood-engraving by Joseph Swain.
182 × 118 mm

In *London Society*, Christmas Number, 1862, p.40.
    The lighthearted poem is unattributed. An idea of its tone may be gained from a short quotation:

> *Oh, happy days! – when love is joy –*
> *Who would not be once more a boy?*

22.   Edward John Poynter, *A Dream of Love*

24. Edward Burne-Jones (1833–1898)
King Sigurd
Wood-engraving by the Dalziel Brothers.
153 × 114 mm

In *Good Words*, 1862, p.248.

Reid wrote: 'The "King Sigurd" is quaint, and perhaps even a little awkward, but in those girls' heads depressed into the picture the artist has already realized the type of feminine beauty he repeated throughout his life . . .' (*Illustrators*, p.100).

The poem, though only given as 'By the author of "The Martyrdom of Kelavane", is the work of an Aberdeen journalist and poet, William Forsyth.

Through smiles and tears, and loving cheers,
And Trumpet notes of fame,
Came King Sigurd, the Crusader, –
Like a conqueror he came.

There stood the noblest of the land,
The pride of many a hall,
But lovely lady Hinda's hand
He kissed before them all.

24.   Edward Burne-Jones, *King Sigurd*

25. Edward Burne-Jones

The Summer Snow
Wood-engraving by the Dalziel Brothers.
144 × 117 mm

In *Good Words*, 1863, facing p.380. Reproduced by Reid facing p.100.

The poem is anonymous. The lines illustrated by Burne-Jones appear in the first verse.

> *Soft falls the summer snow,*
> *On the springing grass drops light,*
> *Not like that which long ago,*
> *Fell so deadly cold and white . . .*

26. Simeon Solomon (1840–1905)

The Feast of Dedication
Wood-engraving by Butterworth and Heath.
94 × 133 mm

In *The Leisure Hour*, 1866, p.73.

Reid was clearly impressed by Solomon's skills as an illustrator. He wrote:'The wood-engravings of Simeon Solomon are not numerous, but some of them are extraordinary . . . If in their individuality one sees the trace of an influence it is that of Rembrandt. The collector will find the ten "Illustrations of Jewish Customs" in the *Leisure Hour* for 1866, and they are so completely unlike anything else that was being done at this time that he cannot afford to ignore them . . . Each one of these drawings is brimmed up with atmosphere strange, sad, exotic, alien . . . It is a beauty created out of what is not beautiful, which may indeed account for its fascination. Its emotion is a kind of nostalgia, a homesickness, a sickness of the soul . . .'(*Illustrators,* pp.103-4).

In the magazine the series was prefaced by the following comment:'We propose to present our readers from time to time with pictures (after drawings executed by Mr Simeon Solomon) of various rites and ceremonies observed by the Jews at the present day in their synagogues and homes. We believe that such illustrations will not be without interest, as they will serve to show in what manner several commandments of the Bible are carried out in practice by this ancient people.'

THE SUMMER SNOW.

25.   Edward Burne-Jones, *The Summer Snow*

S. Solomon.

27.   Simeon Solomon, *The Fast of Jerusalem*

27. Simeon Solomon

The Fast of Jerusalem
Wood-engraving by Butterworth and Heath.
96 × 136 mm

In *The Leisure Hour*, 1866, p.476. Reproduced
by Reid facing p.104.
     Reid remarked of this image:'…in the lights
and shadows of "The Fast of Jerusalem" the
mystery becomes weird, almost disquieting'
(*Illustrators,* p.104).

28. Henry Hugh Armstead (1828–1905)
Sea Weeds
Wood-engraving by the Dalziel Brothers.
139 × 118 mm

In *Good Words*, 1862, p.568.
 Armstead was primarily a sculptor and
made just a handful of designs for wood-
engraving. Reid saw him as essentially a Pre-
Raphaelite and wrote:'The great beauty of
these drawings (for some reason very rarely
mentioned) awakens regret that Armstead made
so few.They are among the most distinguished
our period can boast.' (*Illustrators*, p.107).
 The poem is unattributed.The following
lines give some idea of the tone:

> *We flourish most bright*
> *'Neath the deep rolling wave*
> *Adorning with beauty*
> *Each seaman's lone grave.*
> *Oh, mourners of earth!*
> *Who would deck with sweet flowers*
> *The graves of your loved ones,*
> *Who rest in our bowers . . .*

29. Henry Hugh Armstead
Angel Teachers
Wood-engraving by W.Thomas.
179 × 110 mm

In *Churchman's Family Magazine*, May 1863,
facing p.539.
 One verse of the unattributed poem reads:

> *Sweet teachers by the grave-side met,*
> *My soul to God ye lift,*
> *Who mutely take with grateful hand*
> *The sweets that are his gift;*
> *Nor dread, in blameless innocence,*
> *The sting that comes with time;*
> *But, undismayed, in wonder clasp*
> *The roses of the prime!*

30. Henry Hugh Armstead
Blessed are they that mourn
Wood-engraving by the Dalziel Brothers.
95 × 128 mm

In *The Sunday Magazine*, March 1865, p.409.
 The final verse of the unattributed poem
reads:

> *For God hath marked each sorrowing day*
> *And numbered every secret tear,*
> *And Heaven's long age of bliss shall pay*
> *For all His children suffer here.*

28.   Henry Hugh Armstead, *Sea Weeds*

Chapter 6
Whistler and Charles Keene

31. James McNeill Whistler (1834–1903)
The Trial Sermon
Wood-engraving by the Dalziel Brothers.
151 × 113 mm

In *Good Words*, 1862, p.585. Reproduced by Reid facing p.108.

Reid wrote of Whistler as an illustrator: 'Had we nothing of Whistler's but his six wood-engravings I think we might still claim that he was a great artist. They do not display all his qualities, of course, but they display his poetic imagination, his feeling for decoration, his beauty of line, his sense of composition, and that impeccable taste which in him, as Arthur Symons has said, was carried to the point of genius.' He continued, of this design in particular, '*Her* eyes are fixed upon him, with a wonderful expression of mingled sympathy, affection, and admiration, but *he* is looking into an imaginary world ...' (*Illustrators*, p.108).

The illustration accompanies a story signed 'M.C.' and the relevant passage begins: 'Miss Jemima, the beauty of the family, looked up for a moment from the cushion she had been embroidering for the last two or three years ...'

31.   James McNeill Whistler, *The Trial Sermon*

32. James McNeill Whistler
The Trial Sermon
Wood-engraving by the Dalziel Brothers.
152 × 114 mm

In *Good Words*, 1862, p.649.
   'On this evening she was sitting alone in her little parlour … from her appearance her age must be about twenty-four …'

33. James McNeill Whistler
The Relief Fund in Lancashire
Wood-engraving by an unidentified engraver.
132 × 122 mm

In *Once a Week*, 26 July 1862, p.140.
   The design was intended to accompany an address by Tennyson on the plight of the Manchester cotton weavers who faced destitution because of the lack of raw cotton caused by the American Civil War. In the event Tennyson was too ill to speak at the performance at the Royal Italian Opera, Covent Garden, in aid of the fund, but fortunately the Whistler illustration was retained for publication.

32.   James McNeill Whistler, *The Trial Sermon*

34. Charles Keene (1823–1891)

Mother's Guineas

Wood-engraving by Joseph Swain.

155 × 112 mm

In *The Cornhill Magazine*, July 1864, facing p.1.
Reproduced by Reid facing p.116.

Reid was a passionate admirer of Keene and his collection in Oxford contains more illustrations by him than by any other artist.

The design accompanies a short story by George Eliot entitled *Brother Jacob*. '"Here's the box, Jacob! The box for the guineas!"…When the lozenges were laid bare, he took them out one by one and gave them to Jacob.'

35. Charles Keene

Encouraging

Wood-engraving by an unidentified engraver.

114 × 178 mm

In *Punch*, 22 August 1868, p.86.

Reid wrote: 'To praise these matchless *Punch* pictures is superfluous. Keene never shared the popularity of Leech or du Maurier, or later, of Phil May, though few will deny that he was the greatest of all Mr Punch's artists.' (*Illustrators*, pp.115-16).

MOTHER'S GUINEAS.

34. Charles Keene, *Mother's Guineas*

37.   Frederick Walker, *The Vagrants*

Chapter 7
The Idyllic School

Reid placed in this group Frederick Walker, George Pinwell and John William North.

36. Frederick Walker (1840–1875)
In the November night
Wood-engraving by Joseph Swain.
113 × 156 mm
Reproduced by Reid facing p.146.

In *Good Words*, 1864, facing p.371. One of eleven illustrations which Walker made for Mrs Henry Wood's novel *Oswald Cray*.

Walker had perhaps been over-praised during his tragically short life, not least because he was evidently so charming and attractive a personality. Reid, however, evaluated his talents thoughtfully and remarked, 'there is little imagination in Walker's work; he possessed the type of mind for which the poetic is indistinguishable from the sentimental; therefore we like him best when he contents himself with reproducing charming aspects of ordinary domestic life – a pretty girl shelling peas, or an old woman lifting the kettle from the hob.' (*Illustrators*, p.134).

'The air was keen and frosty, and the flags of the streets were white and clean, as Oswald Cray walked along with Jane Allister in the November night.'

37. Frederick Walker
The Vagrants
Wood-engraving by Joseph Swain.
115 × 168 mm

In *Once a Week*, 27 January 1866, facing p.112.
This appears to be an independent illustration relating to no specific text in the magazine.

38. Frederick Walker
Out among the wild flowers
Wood-engraving by the Dalziel Brothers.
150 × 114 mm

In *Good Words*, 1862, p.657.
Although the poem is apparently 'By a police constable', it is signed 'W.S.F'. This long poem opens:

Ye flowers, that are our silent monitors
At every turn along the changing vale,
From spring-time till the waning of the year …

40. George John Pinwell, *The Gang Children*

39. George John Pinwell (1842–1875)
It contained my picture when I was a boy
Wood-engraving by an unidentified engraver.
152 × 120 mm

In *The Quiver*, 5 January 1867, p.241.
Reproduced by Reid facing p.158.

    Reid wrote of Pinwell's art: 'It is an art
extremely personal in its manner and therefore
in its appeal; it is an art hampered constantly by
an imperfect technique, and yet its very failures
are frequently more interesting than the
successes of cleverer draughtsmen, while its
successes are lovely as April primroses.'
(*Illustrators*, p.152).

    The illustration accompanies 'Home – A
Christmas Story', which is signed 'C.W.S.'

    'I undid the paper. It contained an old gilt
locket. I opened that.

    It contained my picture when I was a boy.
The locket fell from my hands, and I think I
cried out something. The woman lifted up her
veil. It was my mother!'

40. George John Pinwell
The Gang Children
Wood-engraving by the Dalziel Brothers.
132 × 195 mm

In *The Sunday Magazine*, 1 October 1868, p.25.

    The poem by Dora Greenwell deals with the
cruel lot of the children forced to work as farm
labourers.

    Late, late in the evening grey,
    As they trudge on their homeward track
    From the fields where they've worked all day
    You may meet them coming back …

41. George John Pinwell

She is gathering pears in the garden
Wood-engraving by an unidentified engraver.
162 × 120 mm

In *The Quiver*, 29 June 1867, p.641.

The unsigned story, which this design
illustrates, is entitled 'The Soldier of Foxdale'.
Mary Stanford, incorrectly led to believe that
her lover George Leyland has died abroad,
marries the vicar of Foxdale. Ten years later
George returns and although he sees her in the
garden he never reveals himself to her, and 'the
strong man sobbed as he spoke, and gazed
wistfully into the garden'.

'She is gathering pears in the garden, with
her eldest boy; and very bright and cheerful she
looks in the morning sunshine. At times some
memories of the lost George come across her
mind, but they vanish at the thought of her
children and the happiness of her home.'

42. George John Pinwell

Margaret in the Xebec
Wood-engraving by the Dalziel Brothers.
160 × 113 mm

In *Good Words*, 1 April 1870, p.280.
The poem is by Jean Ingelow.

Faultless and fair, all in the moony light,
As one ashamed, she look'd upon the ground,
And her white raiment glisten'd in his sight.
And, hark! the vesper chimes began to sound.

43. George John Pinwell

The Sisters
Wood-engraving by the Dalziel Brothers.
195 × 151 mm

In *The Graphic*, 6 May 1871, p.416.
The poem is signed 'J.A.H.'

Sombre and sad and grim in this our city
To those whose hearts grow faint beneath their toil,
For lack of love or some small grain of pity,
Some little token that in all this coil

Of human life, of human work and thought
Some vein of human sympathy is left;
Some thread of silver delicately wrought
In life's more coarse and roughly woven weft.

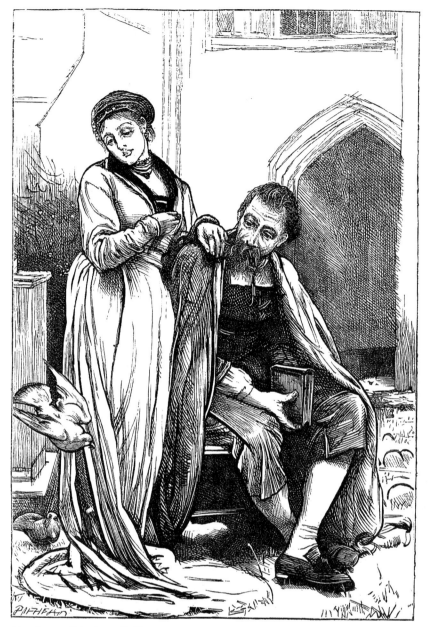

42. George John Pinwell, *Margaret in the Xebec*

Drawn by G. J. Pinwell.   Engraved by Dalziel Brothers.

44.   George John Pinwell, *Think on the Poor*

44. George John Pinwell
Think on the Poor
Wood-engraving by the Dalziel Brothers.
178 × 125 mm

In *The Sunday Magazine*, 1 November 1865,
facing p.104.

   The poem is unattributed.

   Oft lift up the latch of chill Poverty's dwelling,
   Explore the sad chamber where Care sits
      obscure;
   When you see tears of want wash the withering
      bosom,
   Then think of your Saviour and give to the
      poor.

45. John William North (1841–1924)
Autumn Thoughts
Wood-engraving by the Dalziel Brothers.
180 × 116 mm

In *Good Words*, 1863, p.743.
   Reid admired North and saw him as the
greatest of the landscape draughtsmen for
wood-engraving of the period. He wrote: 'To
modern taste North's broader, truer method is
infinitely more satisfying than the painstaking
minuteness of a Birket Foster, but even in his
own day his work never attained popularity, and
was underrated even by his fellow artists ... his
own conscientious, sincere and quiet work was
of a kind that makes its way slowly. His
landscapes are the most beautiful, at once the
broadest and most delicate, that the black and
white art of the sixties can boast.' (*Illustrators*,
pp.163-4).
   The poem is subtitled 'From the German of
Geibel'.

   I saw the forests fade
   The air was still and grey,
   And o'er my soul dismayed
   A heavy sadness lay ...

46. John William North
Winter
Wood-engraving by Joseph Swain.
126 × 170 mm

In *The Sunday Magazine*, February 1865, p.328.
   The text is by the editor of the magazine, Dr
Thomas Guthrie. He used the season as the
starting point of his homily. 'Wrapped in snow,
as an infant in the furs and fleecy coverings a
mother's care provides, the earth is protected
from the severest weather; and, safely sleeping
in her warm bosom, thousands of delicate plants
and animals pass the winter, ready to come
forth at the call of Spring amid the wonders of
an annual resurrection.'

AUTUMN THOUGHTS.

45.   John William North, *Autumn Thoughts*

"FOUNDERED AT SEA."

47.   John William North, *Foundered at Sea*

ASH-WEDNESDAY.

Oft the mourner's wayward heart
Tempts him to hide his grief and die,
Too feeble for Confession's smart,
Too proud to bear a pitying eye

How sweet, in that dark hour, to fall
On bosoms waiting to receive
Our sighs, and gently whisper all?
They love us—will not God forgive?
KEBLE   THE CHRISTIAN YEAR

Drawn by J. D. Watson.

48.   John Dawson Watson, *Ash Wednesday*

47. John William North
Foundered at Sea
Wood-engraving by the Dalziel Brothers.
177 × 128 mm

In *The Sunday Magazine*, 1 January 1867,
facing p.280.
   The poem is unattributed.

The land I knew was a stealthy foe
And a treacherous friend to me;
I looked for ill, and it gave me ill, –
But I trusted in thee, O sea.
   . . .
The faith is shattered, the idol fall'n,
I renounce thee, O traitor sea!
O Thou who rulest the waves and storm,
Mighty Father, I come to Thee.

Chapter 8
John Dawson Watson

48. John Dawson Watson (1832–1892)
Ash Wednesday
Wood-engraving by the Dalziel Brothers.
116 × 188 mm

In *London Society*, March 1862, facing p.150.
Reproduced by Reid facing p.168.
   Reid wrote of Watson:'It will be sufficient . . .
to describe J. D. Watson as a sound
draughtsman, whose work frequently surprises
us by its power and beauty, though nowhere
perhaps does it reveal a very striking
individuality.' (*Illustrators*, p.166).

Although no text in the magazine seems to
be especially illustrated, the design bears the
following from John Keble's *The Christian Year*:

Oft the mourner's wayward heart
Tempts him to hide his grief and die,
Too feeble for Confession's smart,
Too proud to bear a pitying eye.

How sweet, in that dark hour, to fall
On bosoms waiting to receive
Our sighs, and gently whisper all
They love us – will not God forgive?

49. John Dawson Watson

Romance and a Curacy
Wood-engraving by the Dalziel Brothers.
191 × 118 mm

In *London Society*, June 1862, facing p.385.
Reproduced by Reid facing p.170.
    At this point in the unattributed story the young curate ponders on a letter which tells him that his wait for a living will be a long one. He has also just witnessed the death of the woman he had hoped would have become his wife. 'If Margaret had lived, how would he have borne the disappointment of that sentence? And here ended his first and last romance.'

50. John Dawson Watson

The Aspen
Wood-engraving by the Dalziel Brothers.
190 × 118 mm

In *Good Words*, 1863, facing p.401. Reproduced by Reid facing p.166.
    The poem is unattributed.

> *My Darling she nestled quite close to me,*
> *For such shield as mine arms could give her:*
> *'There went not the least waft of wind thro'the*
>   *Tree;*
> *Then why did the aspens shiver?'*

Drawn by J. D. Watson.   p. 398.

ROMANCE AND A CURACY.

49.   John Dawson Watson, *Romance and a Curacy*

Chapter 9
George du Maurier

51. George du Maurier (1834–1896)
Sweet Girl – Graduates ... Afternoon Tea versus Wine
Wood-engraving by Joseph Swain.
176 × 239 mm

In the *Punch Almanack*, 1873.

Reid recognised that, as an illustrator, du Maurier was at his best early in his career and that after 1870, with a few exceptions, his work deteriorated. He wrote: 'This second and more prolific half of du Maurier's career is, for his true admirers, depressing to contemplate. His natural mode of expression was akin to that of the Pre-Raphaelites he satirized so amusingly, and when he abandoned his first manner his work lost its beauty and gained nothing. We no longer get the decorative massing of black on white by which he achieved so rich an effect; detail is sacrificed and delicacy with it; the literary side of his art now comes to be everything, and to present some social triumph of Mrs Ponsonby de Tomkyns gives him greater pleasure than to create a beautiful design.' (*Illustrators*, p.176). Ironically, du Maurier is far better known today as a comic illustrator for *Punch* (as here) and for his novel *Trilby* (1894) than for the work so admired by Reid.

52. George du Maurier
Under the Elm
Wood-engraving by Joseph Swain.
158 × 114 mm

In *Good Words*, 1872, p.605.

The poem is by Isabella Fyvie Mayo and concludes thus:

Sitting under the old elm-tree
Just as I sat seven years ago, –
The western sky in a golden flame,
The twilight meadows stretched out below –
I await that future which brings no pain
To make us long for the Past again.

52. George du Maurier, *Under the Elm*

53. George du Maurier

A Time to Dance
Wood-engraving by the Dalziel Brothers.
140 × 109 mm

In *Good Words*, October 1861, p.579.
The poem is signed 'C.E.' The relevant verse reads:

> *She has stood aloof on her high tower,*
> *To listen, and to prepare*
> *For her Lord: and now, at this last hour,*
> *Shall the Bride make merry there?*
> *Is it yet time to dance?*

54. George du Maurier

Vincent Fleming declares himself
Wood-engraving by Thomas Robinson.
181 × 152 mm

In *The Leisure Hour*, 20 November 1864, p.753.
Reproduced by Reid facing p.172.
Reid wrote: 'These twenty-seven large and comparatively unknown drawings are, in spite of Robinson's mediocre engraving and the poor quality of the paper on which they are printed, in their way almost as fine a series as he ever made for a novel.' (*Illustrators,* p.179).
The story, which is entitled *Hurlock Chase*, is by G. E. Sargent. The relevant passage reads: 'You will excuse me from rising, Rivers: I am very weak, as you see; but not too weak to welcome you, and to say how glad I am to see you once again. Rose has told you why I have sent for you.'…'That you wished to see me, and acknowledge me as your nephew, and yourself as my long-lost uncle, Vincent Fleming.'

55. George du Maurier

Vae Victis
Wood-engraving by Joseph Swain.
156 × 103 mm

In *The Cornhill Magazine*, October 1864, facing p.385.
The novel is *Wives and Daughters* by Elizabeth Gaskell.
'After dinner, too, the gentlemen lingered long over their dessert, and Molly heard them laughing; and then she saw them loitering about in the twilight out-of-doors; Roger hatless, his hands in his pockets, lounging by his father's side, who was now able to talk in his usual loud and cheerful way, forgetting Osborne. *Vae Victis!*'

53.   George du Maurier, *A Time to Dance*

Chapter 10
Arthur Boyd Houghton

56. Arthur Boyd Houghton (1836–1875)
Childhood
Wood-engraving by the Dalziel Brothers.
166 × 94 mm

In *Good Words*, 1863, facing p.636.

Reid wrote of Houghton:'His method is
naturalistic, but the realism of his work is
modified by a temperament impatient of the
obvious, which inclined him to seek the bizarre
and fantastic even in ordinary life. The art of
Houghton and Pinwell is more personal than
that of any other of the younger men, and
attracts or repels with proportionate strength.
Houghton, however, possessed a technique far
beyond that of Pinwell: as a draughtsman at
times he approaches the virtuosity of Charles
Keene.' (*Illustrators,* p.187).

The poem, which is unattributed, deals with
a theme especially dear to the Victorians: that of
childhood, and the contrast between youth and
age in particular.

> *I had no Future then, no Past; my life was
> unto me*
> *But one bright* Now – *the happiness that has
> no History!*
> *Still hath my heart a hearth, but now its circle
> is so wide*
> *That those it burns for, never meet around it
> side by side.*
> *They are severed, they are scattered, and now
> the twilight's fall*
> *Too often only comes to me with shadows on
> the wall.*

57. Arthur Boyd Houghton
Reaping
Wood-engraving by William James Linton.
93 × 126 mm

In *Good Words*, 1 September 1866, between
pp.600 and 601.

One of a group of four designs by Houghton
accompanying a poem signed 'E.A.S.' entitled
'Harvest'.

The first verse reads as follows:

> *Working away at the harvest, reaping the
> ripening grain,*
> *Laying it down in ridges like the men of an
> army slain;*
> *Foremost in toil is the reaper with the sweat on
> his bronzèd brow –*
> *God bless the hand of the reaper, and send him
> vigour enow!*

56. Arthur Boyd Houghton, *Childhood*

59.   Arthur Boyd Houghton, *The Good Samaritan*

58. Arthur Boyd Houghton

The Vision of Sheik Hamil
Wood-engraving by Joseph Swain.
168 × 111 mm

In *The Argosy*, May 1866, usually placed as the
frontispiece to the bound Volume I.
    The poem by Isa Craig appears at pp.500-
503, and opens thus:

> *Up on the terrace Sheik Hamil lay,*
> *In the fort of El-Hamëd, hot in the sun;*
> *But he heeded not the heat of the day*
> *Nor how much of its course had run.*

59. Arthur Boyd Houghton

The Good Samaritan
Wood-engraving by the Dalziel Brothers.
151 × 126 mm

In *The Sunday Magazine*, 1 June 1868, p.552.
    The commentary on the Parable was written
by William Hanna.
    'Gently lifting the body up, and placing it on
his own beast, he moved with gentle pace away.'

Chapter 11
Some Occasional Contributors

60. William Quiller Orchardson
(1836–1910)
One in Every Circle
Wood-engraving by Frederick Borders.
165 × 106 mm

In *Good Words*, 1860, p.648. Reproduced by Reid facing p.200.

Reid wrote: 'Orchardson's few drawings on wood all appeared in *Good Words*, with the exception of one made for *The Sunday Magazine* ... the beauty of several of them is as striking as their originality. "One in every circle" is perhaps the finest; and like the rest is filled with soft silvery greys – grey upon grey, tone melting into tone, the only note of black being in the hair.' (*Illustrators,* p.203).

The poem is signed 'H.M.T.' It opens as follows:

> *A GIRL with something of distress dimming*
> *   her pensive eye,*
> *Who thinks the world must needs be cold to her,*
> *   yet knows not why:*
> *The rapid beating of whose heart shakes not*
> *   her quiet tone,*
> *Who smiles when others smile on her, but*
> *   weepeth when alone ...*

61. John Pettie (1839–1893)
What sent me to Sea
Wood-engraving by the Dalziel Brothers.
148 × 110 mm

In *Good Words*, 1862, p.264. Reproduced by Reid between pp.200 and 203.

Reid describes Pettie as 'that fine illustrator' (*Illustrators,* p.203).

The text is by William Hansard.

'He and I built a whole fleet of ships of every rig, from a frigate to a cutter, over at the carpenter's.'

" He and I built a whole fleet of ships of every rig, from a frigate to a cutter, over at the carpenter's."

61.   John Pettie, *What sent me to Sea*

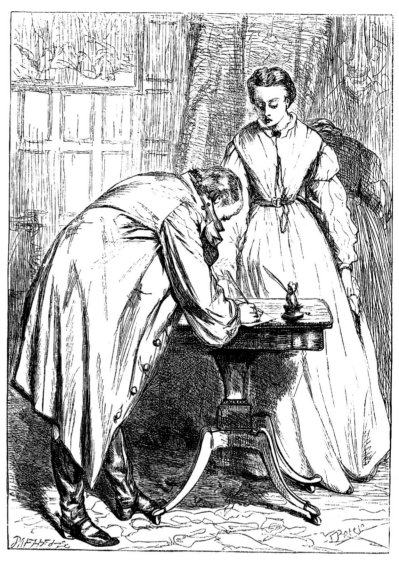

62.   John Pettie, *The Country Surgeon*

62. John Pettie
The Country Surgeon
Wood-engraving by the Dalziel Brothers.
144 × 106 mm

In *Good Words*, 1862, p.713.
    The story is by the Revd Jan de Liefde and
it is set in and around Utrecht.

63.   Thomas Graham, *The Emigrant's Daughter*

63. Thomas Graham (1840–1906)

The Emigrant's Daughter
Wood-engraving by the Dalziel Brothers.
128 × 133 mm

In *Good Words*, August 1861, p.449. Reproduced
by Reid facing p.204.

Graham is little-known as an illustrator and
Reid merely remarked:'Outside the pages of
Good Words I have not met with any drawings
by Tom Graham, but the three designs he
contributed in 1861 to that magazine are all
excellent.' (*Illustrators*, p.204).

The poem is by the author of 'The Patience
of Hope'. The relevant verses read:

> *The gentle light came back to Ellen's eyes,*
> *And to her cheek. 'And is it even thus?'*
> *She said; 'and have you left all other ties –*
> *And have you, William, given up all for us?'*
>
> *And he made answer softly, 'Yes, for you!'*
> *And whispered, as he held her by the hand,*
> *Some words whose sound it seemed to me I knew,*
> *But could not then their import understand . . .*

Drawn by Fred. J. Shields.

Engraved by Swain.

64.   Frederic Shields, *Even as thou wilt*

64. Frederic Shields (1833–1911)
Even as thou wilt
Wood-engraving by Joseph Swain.
125 × 169 mm

In *The Sunday Magazine*, 2 October 1865,
facing p.33.

Reid did not find Shields's illustrations
appealing and merely remarked, arguably a
little harshly, 'I must confess that the work of
Shields does not seem to me to justify the very
high estimation in which it is generally held.'
(*Illustrators,* p.208).

The poem, signed 'C', is based on lines in
St Matthew's Gospel, xv, 22-28. The first verse
reads as follows:

> 'Have mercy on me, Lord!'
> She followed Him, and cried; and, when there came
> No answer, followed, crying still the same, –
> 'Have mercy on me, Lord!'

Chapter 12
T. Morten and William Small

65. Thomas Morten (1836–1866)
The Spirit of Eld
Wood-engraving by the Dalziel Brothers.
181 × 115 mm

In *Good Words*, 1863, facing p.620.

Reid wrote: 'Morten's work has not received the recognition it deserves. It is true that it is uneven, but at its best it is brilliant and highly decorative, with frequently a fantastic element both original and attractive.' (*Illustrators*, p.211).

The story, entitled 'Reminiscences of a Highland Parish', is by Norman Macleod, the editor of *Good Words*. He describes it as '... not an actual transcript of any individual tale but ... one that embodies "the spirit of romance," and presents an example of the general tone and teaching of the old Highland tale, most faithfully and vividly.'

'He followed them through the fire, and not one of the hairs of his head was singed.'

66. Thomas Morten
The Twilight Hour
Wood-engraving by the Dalziel Brothers.
187 × 115 mm

In *Churchman's Family Magazine*, June 1864, facing p.553.

The poem is by Thomas Hood and the first verse reads:

> *Twilight at last! my hour of rest!*
> *The feverish day has sped,*
> *And peace comes, like yon evening star,*
> *that grows from out of the red, –*
> *How pale and white its silvery light*
> *Where sunset's glories spread!*

"He followed them through the fire, and not one of the hairs of his head was singed."

65.   Thomas Morten, *The Spirit of Eld*

67. Thomas Morten

Macdhonuil's Coronach
Wood-engraving by Joseph Swain.
158 × 114 mm

In *Once a Week*, 28 January 1865, p.161.
Reproduced by Reid, p.210.

The poem is by William Black. The last two verses read:

> *On gloomy hill-side, red and sere*
> *There rests a lonely grave:*
> *There lay they him, where he may hear*
> *By night the dark sea rave.*
>
> *And for her love pale Ellen weeps,*
> *Forsaken and alone;*
> *While Ian on the hill-side sleeps*
> *Beneath the cold, grey stone.*

67.   Thomas Morten, *Macdhonuil's Coronach*

68. William Small (1843–1929)

Between the Cliffs
Wood-engraving by J. Williamson.
164 × 118 mm

In *The Quiver*, 25 November 1865, p.153.

Reid called Small 'a brilliant and powerful draughtsman, a master in his own manner …' (*Illustrators*, p.217).

The final verse of the poem which is signed 'F.J.F.', reads as follows:

> Dead and alone,
>   By the trysting-stone:
> Cold and dead, as the dastard heart
> Of him who left her alone with the smart
> Of a mocking world; cold and dead,
> As the withered wreath around her head!
>   And the river, fleet,
>   Bathes her weary feet;
> And the lightning's flash is her winding sheet.

69. William Small

Lilies
Wood-engraving by the Dalziel Brothers.
166 × 113 mm

In *Good Words*, 1 December 1866. Usually placed as the frontispiece to the bound volume for 1866. Reproduced by Reid facing p.216.

The design acccompanies a poem by the Revd H. R. Haweis. The final verse reads:

> And I often dream of the valleys
> Long ago, and the sweet spring-tide,
> And the little stream and the lilies,
> And the maiden that stood beside.

"LILIES."

69.   William Small, *Lilies*

"GRIFFITH GAUNT."

70.   William Small, Untitled illustration to Charles Reade's *Griffith Gaunt*

70. William Small
Untitled illustration to *Griffith Gaunt*
Wood-engraving by Joseph Swain.
106 × 158 mm

In *The Argosy*, October 1866, facing p.345.
Reproduced by Reid facing p.322.
    The design illustrates a scene in chapter 41
of *Griffith Gaunt* by Charles Reade. Mrs Gaunt,
in despair, 'began to doubt and to despond …
She placed her crucifix at the foot of the wall,
and laid herself down on the ground and kissed
His feet, then drawing back, gazed upon that
effigy of the mortal sufferings of our Redeemer.'

Chapter 13
A Miscellaneous Group

71. John Lawson (*fl.* 1865–1909)
The Earl o' Quarterdeck
Wood-engraving by Joseph Swain.
157 × 117 mm

In *The Argosy*, January 1866, facing p.147.
Reproduced by Reid facing p.228.

Reid wrote of Lawson that he 'is not among the greater artists of our period, but his work is often good, and at its best is distinguished by a purity of line and a pleasing use of rich solid blacks' (*Illustrators,* p.228).

The poem, which is unattributed, is described simply as 'A New Old Ballad'. The two relevant verses are as follows:

> *Quo the skipper: 'Ye are a lady fair,*
> *And a princess grand to see;*
> *But ye are a woman, and a man wad sail*
> *To hell in yer company.'*
> *. . .*
> *But she took na her han' frae the good ship's helm,*
> *Until the day did daw;*
> *And the skipper he spak, but what he said*
> *It was said atween them twa*

"AND THE SKIPPER HE SPAK, BUT WHAT HE SAID
IT WAS SAID ATWEEN THEM TWA."

71.   John Lawson, *The Earl o' Quarterdeck*

72. Samuel Luke Fildes (1844–1927)

Cassandra
Wood-engraving by Joseph Swain.
155 × 103 mm

In *Once a Week*, 21 September 1867, facing
p.345.

Reid felt that Fildes did not perhaps fulfil
his early promise, chiefly because his arrival as
an illustrator came a little late. 'What gave the
artist his best chance was the custom of
illustrating in both books and magazines brief
pieces in prose and verse, and that custom has
now practically ceased.' (*Illustrators*, p.237). He
praised 'Cassandra' for its 'power' and remarked
on the 'tenderness' of no.73, 'Feuilles d'Automne'
(*Illustrators*, p.236).

The poem, by J. Mew, opens as follows:

> *Alone, she wanders over Até's hills*
> *Crowned with a thousand herds, the prophetess*
> *Cassandra, the pale violet of Troy,*
> *Fairest of Priam's daughters; slow, sweet, songs*
> *Of siren's music, mournful melodies,*
> *Her white lips covered with the laurel foam,*
> *Singing alone . . .*

73. Samuel Luke Fildes

Feuilles d'Automne
Wood-engraving by Joseph Swain.
146 × 110 mm

In *Once a Week*, 7 September 1867, p.285.
The poem, signed 'C.R.B.', is described as
being 'From Victor Hugo'. It opens as follows:

> *In dark recess, hard by the spot*
> *Whence mother's prayer arises night and day,*
> *Sheltered within his tiny cot*
> *A lovely infant sleeping lay . . .*

74. Edward Linley Sambourne

(1845–1910)
Cover design for the *Punch Almanack*, 1896
Wood-engraving by Joseph Swain.
216 × 198 mm

Reid admired Sambourne and wrote: '. . .
Sambourne's technique developed rapidly . . . he
himself said that he formed his style on that of
Albert Dürer – deliberately making it as simple
as possible however; giving the engraver little or
no cross-hatching to do, and relying for effects
on single lines of varying thickness. The beauty
he achieved was largely a beauty of decoration
and silhouette, but he learned to draw the
human body with a wonderful purity of line
and grace of modelling.' (*Illustrators*, p.238).

72. Samuel Luke Fildes, *Cassandra*

74. Edward Linley Sambourne, cover design for the *Punch Almanack*, 1896

Chapter 14
The Rank and File: With Some New Recruits

75. Frederick Richard Pickersgill
(1820–1900)
The Wishing Well; or, Christmas-Time at Langton Hall
Wood-engraving by Edmund Evans.
193 × 117 mm

In *London Society*, Christmas Number, 1862, facing p.28.

Reid wrote: '. . . Pickersgill's work is always that of an artist, never the careless journalism which some more brilliant draughtsmen were content to produce.' (*Illustrators*, p.251).

The story is unattributed.

'To it the lads and lasses of the neighbouring villages go to pledge their mutual vows firmly believing that heaven has a peculiar blessing for those whose faith is plighted beside the Holy Well.'

Drawn by F. R. Pickersgill, R.A.   p. 28.

75.   Frederick Richard Pickersgill, *The Wishing Well; or, Christmas-Time at Langton Hall*

76. James Mahoney (1847–79)
Autumn Tourists
Wood-engraving by Edward Whymper.
158 × 107 mm

In *The Argosy*, August 1866, facing p.217.
Reid wrote: 'His [Mahoney's] life seems to
have been a passionate and disreputable one,
haunted no doubt by visions of an utterly
different kind, but of which we can know
nothing. It ended sordidly in a public latrine.
His work is as wayward as his life, and probably
reflects its violent reactions.' (*Illustrators*, p.255).
The poem is signed 'D.W.' The first two
verses read:

> *They were rowing over a summer lake,*
> *A lake deep blue and without a curl,*
> *Save just the ripple the oars would make,*
> *And the shoreward streak of pearl.*
>
> *High over the water the mountains rise,*
> *Deep under the water the mountains fall;*
> *You may fathom the depths and mete the skies,*
> *But the heart is deeper than all.*

77. Robert Barnes (1840–1895)
A surprise
Wood-engraving by Joseph Swain.
157 × 110 mm

In *The Cornhill Magazine*, September 1864,
facing p.257.
Reid saw Barnes's qualities as rather limited
and accused him of an 'absence of imagination'
and a 'preference for a somewhat bovine type of
beauty'. However, he was typically acute when
he wrote: 'Barnes would have been the right
man to illustrate George Eliot's earlier novels; he
would have been the wrong man to illustrate the
novels of Mr Hardy.' (*Illustrators*, pp.256-7).
The story illustrated is *Margaret Denzil's
History* by Frederick Greenwood.
'I beg your pardon, Margaret,' he said, and
turned about, and set *his* eyes also on the
surprising figure in the doorway. They met hers:
at the same instant, smoothing the folds of her
rustling dress, she made him a low, profound,
sarcastic obeisance, such as I well remembered
to have seen before.'

78. Robert Barnes
'*"Puir Thing!" said the washerwoman*'
Wood-engraving by Joseph Swain.
158 × 114 mm

In *Good Words*, 1865, facing p.208. Reproduced
by Reid facing p.258.
The novel is *Alfred Hagart's Household* by
Alexander Smith.
' A washerwoman who happened to be
passing laid down her basket of clothes, and
with the instinct of her sex came to the rescue.'

" AUTUMN TOURISTS."

76.   James Mahoney, *Autumn Tourists*

79. Mary Ellen Edwards (1839–*c*.1910)
Cuckoo!
Wood-engraving by the Dalziel Brothers.
156 × 100 mm

In *The Argosy*, July 1866, facing p.129.

Reid wrote that Edwards 'would occupy a higher position among our illustrators had she not repeated herself so monotonously. But whether she is picturing one of the lugubrious scenes in Foxe's *Book of Martyrs*, or a mildly sentimental scene from some innocent love tale, she gives us always precisely the same pretty maiden. Yet she had, in her own small way, a genuine talent, and her work in the beginning was interesting.' (*Illustrators,* p.261).

The poem is by John Banks and the final lines read as follows:

> *And I sicken and sigh,*
> *With my heart thrill'd through,*
> *And wherever I fly*
> *I hear the cry –*
> *'Cuckoo!'*

80. Helen Allingham (1848–1926)
She took up her position as directed
Wood-engraving by Joseph Swain.
104 × 159 mm
And an initial letter 'P'

In *The Cornhill Magazine*, June 1874, facing p.641 (larger design) and also on p.641 (initial's design).

Reid did not deal with Allingham in his study. The block is signed in the artist's maiden name of Paterson. It was while at work on this project in August 1874 that she married the poet William Allingham and later blocks bear the new surname. Hardy wrote to Edmund Gosse that Allingham was 'the best illustrator I ever had'.

The text is Hardy's *Far From the Madding Crowd* and it appeared in this periodical prior to its publication in book form. The scene is the celebrated swordplay of Sergeant Troy with the heroine, Bathsheba Everdene.

THE CUCKOO.

79. Mary Ellen Edwards, *Cuckoo!*

Notes on Contributors

Colin Harrison is an Assistant Keeper in the Department of Western Art, Ashmolean Museum, Oxford.

Brian Taylor is a Lecturer in the School of Cultural and Community Studies, Sussex University. He has written extensively on Forrest Reid and is the author of *The Green Avenue: the life and writings of Forrest Reid, 1875-1947* (Cambridge University Press, 1980).

Christopher Fitz-Simon is a former Literary Manager and Artistic Director of the National Theatre Society (Abbey and Peacock Theatres). His principal books are *The Irish Theatre* (Thames & Hudson), *The Arts in Ireland* (Gill & Macmillan), and *The Boys* (Nick Hern/Heinemann), the biography of Hilton Edwards and Michael MacLiammoir. He is the author of a large number of broadcast plays, and has dramatised Forrest Reid's *The Bracknels* as a six-part serial.

Norman Vance is Professor of English in the School of English and American Studies, Sussex University. He is the author of *Irish Literature, a social history: tradition, identity and difference* (Oxford, Blackwell, 1990).

John McGahern was the first prose writer to receive the A. E. Memorial Award (1962). His first novel, *The Barracks*, was published in 1962 and his other acclaimed books include *The Dark* (1965), *Nightlines* (1970), *The Leavetaking* (1974), *Getting Through* (1978), *The Pornographer* (1979) and *Amongst Women* (1990). Mr McGahern's article 'Brian Westby' first appeared in *Threshold* No. 28 (Spring 1977) and is reproduced with kind permission of the Lyric Theatre, Belfast.

Angela Thirlwell is a lecturer in Literature for the Extra-Mural Centre, Birkbeck College, London University. She is the editor of *The Folio Anthology of Autobiography* (1994) and wrote the introduction and epilogue to *The Pre-Raphaelites and their World* (1995). She is currently writing a joint biography of William Michael Rossetti and Lucy Madox Brown Rossetti.

Robin de Beaumont is an antiquarian bookseller with a special interest in the nineteenth century. In 1992 he gave his notable collection of illustrated books of the 1860s to the Department of Prints and Drawings at the British Museum. He is currently President of The Private Libraries Association.

Paul Goldman was formerly an Assistant Keeper in the Department of Prints and Drawings in the British Museum and is now an antiquarian bookseller. He is the author of *Victorian Illustrated Books – The Heyday of Wood-engraving* (1994) and *Victorian Illustration – The Pre-Raphaelites, The Idyllic School and The High Victorians* (1996).

Anne Harvey is a distinguished compiler of poetry anthologies who also gives readings throughout the country and on radio. She has a special interest in poetry intended for children and is an expert on, amongst others, Edward Thomas, Eleanor Farjeon and Christina Rossetti.

Robert Greacen is one of Ireland's most highly regarded poets. His *Collected Poems 1944-1994* have been published by the Lagan Press. His essay 'Tomorrow Evening About Eight' is Chapter 14 of a volume of autobiography *Even Without Irene* (1969, Dolmen Press. Reprinted 1995, Lagan Press) and is reprinted here with permission.

Index of Artists

Figures in **bold** indicate illustrations reproduced here.

Index of Illustrations

Figures in **bold** indicate illustrations reproduced here.